- Note from the Publisher

Welcome to a glimpse into the world of international ... for you to be able to explore beyond the boundaries of ... other fiber artists are doing.

In many countries, rather than learning from various ... a single master, spending years progressing from simple techniques to the ... Intricate designs are celebrated and sewing and quilting by hand is honored and as such, ... quilting is the typical method used to quilt.

This book was written in its original language, Japanese, by a master quilter, Yoko Saito. We have done our best to make the directions for each project easy to understand if you have some level of quilting experience, while maintaining the appearance and intent of the original author and publisher.

We hope the beautifully designed handmade items in this book inspire and encourage you to make them for yourself.

- Important Tips Before You Begin -

These facts might suggest that intermediate or advanced quilters will be more comfortable working on these projects.

- Techniques -

Certain detailed descriptions of specific techniques in earlier projects are not repeated in later projects. It is advisable to read through the book from the beginning, even if making a project that appears later in the book, as earlier projects may describe key techniques in detail.

- Measurements -

The original designs were created using the metric system for dimensions. In order to assist you, we have included the imperial system measurements in brackets. However, please note that samples that appear in the book were created and tested using the metric system. Thus, you will find that if you use the imperial measurements to make the projects, the items you make will not be exactly the same size as when using the metric measurements. Please also note that seam allowances are called out in separately and highlighted in boxes.

- Patterns/Templates -

Patterns for each project appear in several different ways: a) as dimensional diagrams b) in the pattern sheet inserts c) in the body of the text d) illustrations. One must read through all the instructions carefully to understand what size to cut the fabric and related materials including instructions for each project relating to seam allowances.

Stitch Publications, 2013

Yoko Saito's

Strolling Along Paths of Green

Forward

I love the tender green color of plants I see in nature.

Although I live in the city, there are many parks and green areas in my neighborhood. There are the beautiful gardens of nearby houses and the rolling green banks along the river.

On my daily walk with our family dog, my eyes are drawn to the brightly colored flowers and the small, delicate pale green plants.

In the world of quilting, there are distinct designs and use of colors. However, not many represent the hues and intricate shapes of Mother Nature. It gives me great pleasure to bring together shades of my favorite greens and nature's motifs in a quilt.

Although it is beyond my power to do nature justice, my goal was to stay faithful to it in each design. To create with one's own hands means leaving one's mark in the world, and that is a positive thing. Combining nature's unparalleled designs with your own handwork will result in beautiful and charming quilts, handbags and other items for you to use and admire for many years. Now, let's go for a stroll in search of beautiful plants from which we can begin to design quilts and other projects inspired by nature.

Yoko Saito

Table of Contents

Plants through the Four Seasons

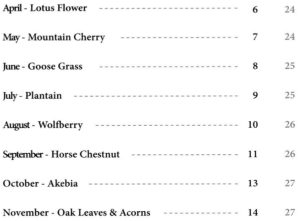

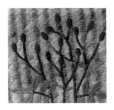

Strolling with Greenery — Bags & Pouches" —

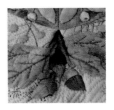

The Quilted Woods

Plants through the Four Seasons

During my daily walk, it's the plants that tell me of the changing seasons. I love to bask in the warm spring sunshine while spying plants coming to life. Throughout the seasons, their appearance and colors continue to change.

April - Lotus Flower

The small blooms resemble the lotus. That is why, in Japanese, the plant is named for it. The small, round leaves are perfect for beginners to learn the basics of appliqué .

----- instructions p. 24

6

May - Mountain Cherry

Wild mountain cherry trees flower at different times depending on their variety.   I find great delight in the intricate variations of the blooming flowers of these trees.   Carefully choose the colors of your fabrics in order to bring out the delicate pink shades of the blossoms against the background.

----- instructions p. 24

June - Goose Grass

As the Chinese name for this plant, "Eight Branch Stalks", suggests, the many stems and branches grow out of one main stalk. The 6-8 leafy stems grow in a thickly-layered ring. Use your needle to turn the curves of each appliquéd leaf under a little at a time as you stitch.

----- instructions p 25

Alternate Pattern >>>

July - Plantain

Undaunted by being tread upon, this resilient plant often grows through cracks in asphalt.   Use the colonial knot stitch to outline and fill in the blooms.

----- instructions p. 25

August - Wolfberry

The wolfberry, also called the goji berry, is known for its health benefits.
The bright red fruit is typically dried and used in cooking. The leaves and
root bark are also thought to be medicinally beneficial. Select the vibrant
red of the fruit; the delicate pink of the flower.

----- instructions p. 26

September - Horse Chestnut

Also known by its French name, "marronnier", this tree is often planted along streets and boulevards. I love the prickly surface of the chestnut hull. The appliqué pattern is fairly large so choose a background fabric that will enhance the overall design.

----- instructions p. 26

Alternate Design >>>

Lotus Flower

Mountain Cherrry

Plantain

Wolfberry

October - Akebia

Coming across this plant on a walk always brings a
smile to my face. The fruit is vaguely sweet, and the
vine is often used in basket-making for it's depths of color, which, for
one who loves baskets, appeals to me. Appliqué the complex design by
intertwining the vines.

----- instructions p. 27

November - Oak Leaves & Acorns

Sawtooth Oaks, Kashi Oaks, Nara Oaks; the acorns of each have different shapes and aspects, which I find so interesting upon comparison. To appliqué the curves with ease, snip into the seam allowance "v" of each of the indents around the lobes of the leaves.

----- instructions p. 27

Alternate Design >>>

December - Mistletoe

Mistletoe is an unusual plant that lives on host trees, such as the Beech or Zelkova, and absorbs nutrients and moisture from them. The stems and leaves remind me of a whirligig made out of bamboo. Arrange the layering of the pieces as you stitch, overlapping for a more natural look.

----- Instructions p. 28

January - Shepherd's Purse

Ever since I was a little girl, I would often pull this plant out of the ground and shake it vigorously from the stem to hear a lovely rustling sound. Appliquéing the small pieces that make up the blooms takes quite a bit of patience, but the results are rewarding.

----- Instructions p. 28

February - Peas

The small pea pods and rounded leaves undulate gently in the breeze as the plant grows upward. While the various shapes are unique, I especially like the beautiful little flowers. The curling vines are embroidered with the smallest possible of outline stitches.

----- instructions p. 29

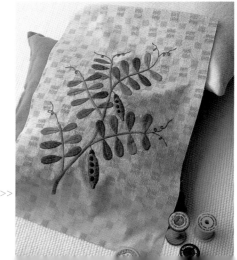

Alternate Design >>>

March -- Clover

Clover is another favorite plant. Perhaps because there is a wonderful legend where one who finds a four-leaf clover finds happiness. Is there anyone who hasn't made a garland or crown from the flowers when they were little? The flower, made of embroidered rows of straight stitches, will appear softer if the stitches are uneven.

----- Instructions p. 29

Akebia

Mistletoe

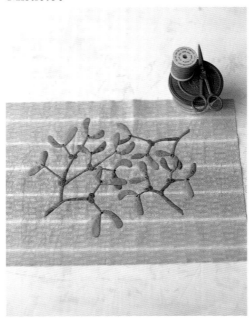

Shepherd's Purse

Clover

Quilting Basics

The following quilting and appliqué techniques, shown in Basics 1-11, are used throughout this book in the designs and patterns in each of the 12 months. Refer to these tutorials as needed.

Basics 1	Making Individual Bias Strips

1 Lay fabric on the non-slip board and fold down at an angle, using the markings on your ruler to achieve a perfect 45° angle.

2 Fold the fabric back up, keeping the ruler at a 45° angle. Using a chalk pencil, draw the first marking line that will be used as a reference line. Draw additional cutting lines parallel to the reference line in intervals of 1 cm [⅜"].

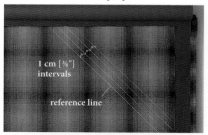

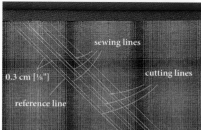

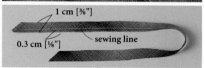

3 Draw sewing lines 0.3 cm [⅛"] away from each cutting line. Cut the fabric apart on the marked cutting lines to create a 1 cm [⅜"] wide bias strip.

Basics 2	Making Bias Strips for Binding

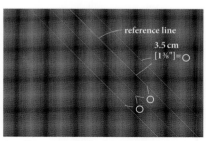

1 Follow steps 1 and 2 from Basics 1, but draw the cutting lines at 3.5 cm [1⅜"] intervals from the reference line.

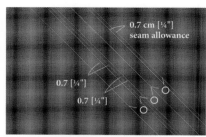

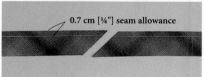

2 Draw sewing lines 0.7 cm [¼"] away from each cutting line. Cut the fabric apart on the marked cutting lines to create a 3.5 cm [1⅜"] wide bias strip.
* The accuracy of the marked seam allowance (sewing lines) are critical to make sure that the bias binding is straight when sewing the strips together.

Basics 3	Sewing Bias Strips Together for Binding

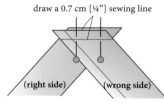

1 Take 2 bias strips and lay them crossed with right sides together, to create right angles. Match the edges. Draw a 0.7 cm [¼"] sewing line to mark the seam allowance.

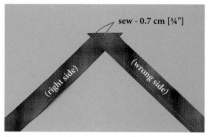

2 Sew across the 2 strips on the marked sewing line by hand or by machine.

3 Trim the rabbit ears off of the binding at each seam. Make enough continuous binding to equal the length needed for the project.

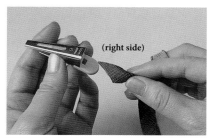

(right side)

1 Feed the 1.5 cm [⅝"] bias strip or binding into the bias tape maker right side up. Guide it along with a needle until it emerges from the other end.

(wrong side)

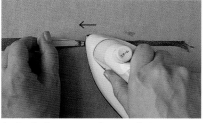

2 Flip the bias tape maker upside down. Press the folded bias binding with the tip of the iron and gently pull the bias tape maker away from the iron. As you pull away, iron the folded bias tape that appears. Continue this along the entire length.

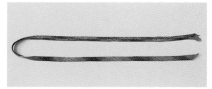

3 The 0.6 cm [¼"] bias tape is completed.

cut off the seam allowance on this side

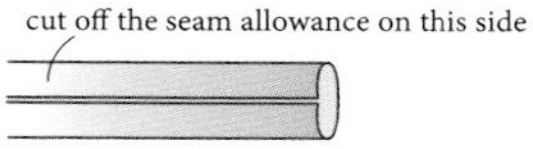

1 Taking the 0.6 cm [¼"] bias tape created in Basics 4, carefully cut off one side of the folded seam allowance at the fold line.

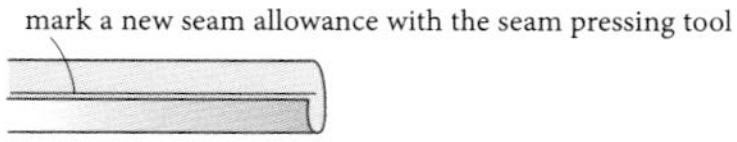

mark a new seam allowance with the seam pressing tool

2 Use the seam pressing tool to mark a new sewing line where the remaining seam allowance meets when folded.

fold down

0.3~0.4

3 Fold down the seam allowance created in step 2 and with the seam pressing tool, press firmly again from the top. The 0.3 - 0.4 cm [⅛"~ ¼"] bias tape is completed.

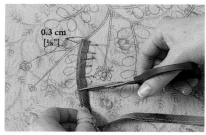

0.3 cm [⅛"]

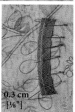

0.3 cm [⅛"]

1 Take a length of 0.3 - 0.4 cm [⅛"~ ¼"] bias strip and pin in place on the marked background fabric, matching the fold line to the drawn pattern. Trim the end of the strip, leaving 0.3 cm [⅛"] for the seam allowance.

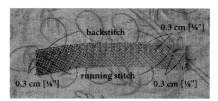

backstitch   0.3 cm [⅛"]

0.3 cm [⅛"]   running stitch   0.3 cm [⅛"]

2 Using a running stitch, begin and end stitches 0.3 cm [⅛"] from the ends. Backstitch at either end to secure the stitches in place.

3 Fold the bias strip over right side out and finger press the stem into place.

0.3 cm [⅛"]   blindstitch   0.3 cm [⅛"]

4 Turn the edge of the bias strip under, the width of the stem, as drawn on the background fabric. Appliqué the stem down to within 0.3 cm of each end.

Basics 7. Appliquéing Stems (with the grain)

1 Place the branch along the grain of the right side of the fabric and mark the outline of the pattern. Add a 0.3 cm [⅛"] seam allowance. Cut it out. Pin the branch to the background fabric matching the marked area.

2 Appliqué from the top of the branches, turning under the seam allowance with the tip of the needle as you go.

3 Appliqué to the corner of the branch, then carefully fold the seam allowance under to form the bottom and appliqué to the next corner. Trim the rabbit ear.

4 Take 3 tiny stitches as you turn the seam allowance under to get a sharp corner.

5 Continue stitching the sides of the branch, as shown in step 3, leaving the top of the branch end open (this will be covered later by the leaves).

Basics 8. Appliquéing Rounded Pieces

1 Mark the outline of the design on the right side of the fabric. Cut out the appliqué pieces with a 0.3 cm [⅛"] seam allowance and pin in position.

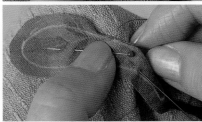

2 Begin to appliqué half-way along the outer curve, turning the seam allowance under with the tip of the needle as you go.

3 Make five snips along the inner curve, making sure to stay within the seam allowance.

4 Turn the seam allowance under as you continue appliquéing the piece completely down.

Basics 9 — Appliquéing V-Shapes

1 Mark the outline of the design on the right side of the fabric. Cut out the appliqué pieces with a 0.3 cm [⅛"] seam allowance and pin in position.

2 Begin to appliqué along the side where it gently curves to within 2-3 stitches of the top of the heart shape. Make one snip within the "v" of the seam allowance.

3 Turn the snipped seam allowance under with the tip of the needle.

4 Since there is no seam allowance where the snip was made, bring the tip of the needle to the front and take at least two tiny stitches to secure the inverted point. Continue to appliqué around the edge.

5 Trim the rabbit ear.

6 Divide the appliquéing of v-shaped pieces into two steps: 1)starting at a gentle curve and stitching to the "v", and 2) appliquéing from the point of the "v" back to where you began.

Basics 10 — Appliquéing Edge-folded Pieces

(right side)

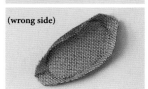
(wrong side)

1 Place and mark your pattern on the wrong side of the piece, adding 0.3 cm [⅛"] seam allowance. Using a seam pressing tool, press hard along the pattern line to create a fold. Turn the piece over and finger press the seam allowance.

2 Taking the folded edge appliqué that you created in step 1, pin in place on the background fabric. Blindstitch the appliqué piece down in position.

Basics 11 — Appliquéing Overlapping Pieces

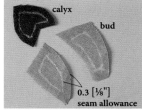
calyx
bud
0.3 [⅛"]
seam allowance

1 Mark the outline of the design on the right side of the fabric. Cut out the appliqué pieces with a 0.3 cm [⅛"] seam allowance.

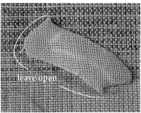
leave open

2 Appliqué the bottom-most piece first, leaving open where the next piece overlaps on top.

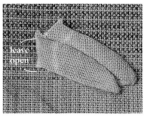
leave open

3 Overlap the next bud, being sure to cover the open edge underneath. Stitch down leaving edges open on the end.

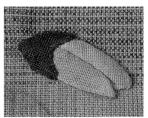

4 Place the calyx in position to cover the open edge and appliqué all the way around the piece while turning under the seam allowance. Refer to the steps in Basics 9 if necessary.

General Directions - Month by Month

- April - Lotus Flower

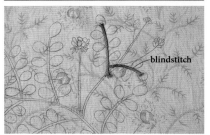

1 To appliqué the stems, cut them to length referring to the pattern drawn on the background fabric (Basics 6).

2 Appliqué the shorter stems first, trimming the inside edges within the drawn lines of the longest central stems (as these open ends will be covered by the longer stems).

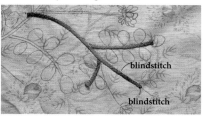

blindstitch
blindstitch

3 Overlap and appliqué the central stem (covering the open ends of the short stems from step 2) turning under the seam allowance 0.3 cm [⅛"].

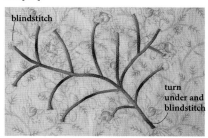

blindstitch

turn under and blindstitch

4 As in steps 1~3 above, appliqué all of the shorter stems first, followed by the longer, central stems. Turn under all seam allowances 0.3 cm [⅛"].

flower (A)

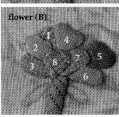

flower (B)

5 For flowers A and B, begin to appliqué pieces in numerical order, leaving edges open where the next pieces will overlap.

6 Refer to the steps in Basics 10 for details on how to appliqué edge-folded leaves.

bud

7 Embroider the roots, buds and veins on the leaves (refer to p. 65 for embroidery instructions).

- May - Mountain Cherry

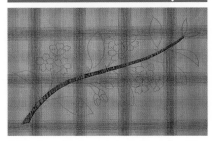

1 The branches are cut along the grain of the fabric. Snip several times along the sharper curve areas within the seam allowance (Basics 7).

2 To appliqué the flowers, follow the steps for v-shaped appliqués in Basics 9 and appliquéing buds in Basics 11.

3 Use the folded-edge appliqué technique to make and appliqué down the leaves (Basics 10).

4 Embroider the center of the flowers, calyx, veins and stems.

- June -
Goose Grass

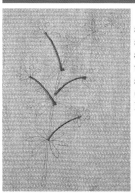

1 Make the bias strips for the stems (Basics 1), and appliqué the short, side stems first. (April - Lotus Flower).

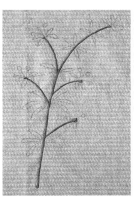

2 Next, appliqué the center stem (Basics 6). Appliqué the bottom edge of the stem, but leave the top edge open.

3 Appliqué the leaves in order, starting with the smallest and working up to the largest (Basics 8).

4 Finally, appliqué the berries (Basics 8), and embroider the stems and veins on the leaves.

- July -
Plantain

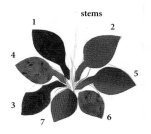

1 Appliqué leaves 1~4, the flower stems, and then the remaining leaves, 5~7.

2 Make 3 small snips in the seam allowance on either side of the "v". Use a seam pressing tool to press the seam allowances in (Basics 10).

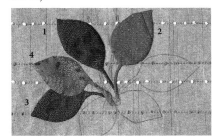

3 Place leaf 1 in position on the drawn pattern. Appliqué around the leaf, leaving the bottom of the stem open. Continue with leaves 2~4 in order, overlapping as shown.

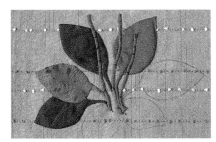

4 Referring to the pattern, draw the location for the flower stems. Cut bias strips for the stems (Basics 1). Appliqué them in place, leaving the top and bottom ends open (Basics 6).

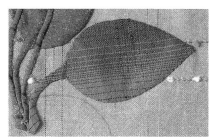

5 If the base of the leaf is at a sharper angle than 90°, snip into the seam allowance for ease as you appliqué. Turn the seam allowance with the tip of the needle as you go, taking 3 tiny stitches at the inside corner to secure (Basics 9).

6 Leaves 6 and 7 will overlap and cover the open ends of the leaves and stems.

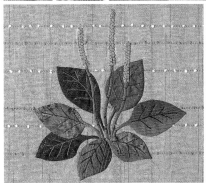

7 Make the flowers at the top of the stems using a colonial knot stitch. Then, outline stitch the veins on the leaves.

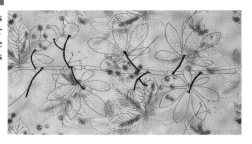

1   Appliqué the shorter twigs first, using bias strips (Basics 1). Then appliqué the longer ones down, overlapping the open ends of the shorter twigs (Basics 6) until all of the twigs are completed.

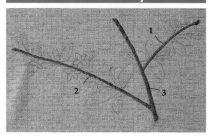

1   Cut bias strips for the branches (Basics 1), and appliqué them in order from 1~3 (Basics 6).

2   Draw the pattern on the right side of the fabric for the thicker branches and cut them out with a 0.3 cm [⅛"] seam allowance. Then make two 4 x 1.2 cm [1½" x ½"] branch sections cut on the bias.

3   Referring to Basics 6 and the drawn pattern, appliqué the branch sections to the background first.

2   For the leaves, draw the pattern on the right side of the fabric pieces and use the tip of the needle to turn the seam allowance under while appliquéing (Basics 8). Fold the tips of the leaves under in 2 steps (Basics 7).

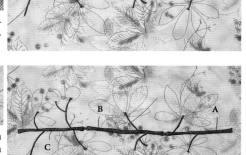

4   Next, appliqué the thicker branches in place, matching up the marks. Turn the seam allowance under with the tip of the needle as you go and appliqué all the way around the branch.

3   Appliqué the flowers and buds (Basics 11).

5   Draw the pattern on the right side of the fabric for the leaves and use a seam pressing tool to press the seam allowance to the wrong side (Basics 10). Start appliquéing the bottommost leaves, making crisp corners (Basics 7).

4   Embroider the veins in the leaves, the centers of the flowers, the lines on the buds and the stems.

6   Appliqué the nuts and hulls (Basics 11). Embroider v-shaped straight stitches in a random pattern over the nuts and hulls. Embroider veins on the leaves.

- October -
Akebia

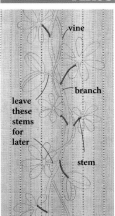

1 Cut bias strips for the stems (Basics 1), and appliqué them in position as drawn onto the background (Basics 6). Only appliqué the ones shown to the left. The remaining will be done later.

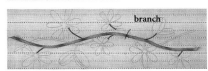

2 Make 1 branch and 2 sections of vine (Basics 4 and 5). Position the branch in place.

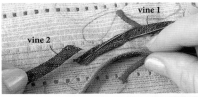

3 Entwine the vines with the branch, referring to the design. At the end of vine 1, overlap vine 2 by 0.5 cm [¼"] and pin it down. Continue to lay the vine in place. Baste down the center of both sections of the vine and the branch.

4 Begin to appliqué from the lower-left of the branch near the corner (Basics 7), and stitch all the way around the branch. In the spots (A and B) where the vine overlaps the stems, leave an opening the width of a stem (as these stems will be inserted and appliquéd later). In places where the vine goes over the branch, tie off and knot your thread on the wrong side. Begin again on the other side of the vine. Once the branch is completely appliquéd down, go back and do both sections of the vine.

5 Appliqué the leaves (Basics 10) onto the stems that are there, but not the ones that are left for later.

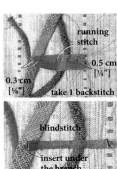

6 Appliqué the stems that were left until later (A). Referring to Basics 6, stitch them in place, lifting up the spaces left in the branch with the tip of the needle and inserting the ends of the stems under the branch.

7 Go back and blindstitch the sections of the branch that were left open for the stems. Next, appliqué the stems for the fruit (B) in the same way as above.

8 Appliqué the remaining leaves in place; then, the fruit (Basics 11); embroider the veins on the leaves.

- November -
Oak Leaves & Acorns

1 Draw the pattern on the right side of the fabric for the leaves and cut the appliqué pieces out with a 0.3 cm [⅛"] seam allowance. Begin to appliqué from the leaf in the lower right corner of the design, starting with the stem. Snip into the seam allowance in the indents of each lobe. Turn the seam allowance under with the tip of the needle as you go (Basics 9).

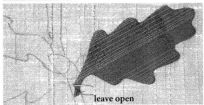

2 Appliqué around the lobes of the leaf (Basics 9). Appliqué the remaining leaves.

3 Next, appliqué the branch, referring to Basics 7. Then, appliqué the acorns (Basics 11), and finally, embroider the veins onto the leaves and the buds on the branch.

27

- December -
Mistletoe

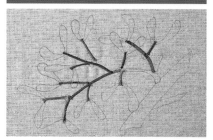

1 Cut the twigs from bias strips (Basics 1), and appliqué the bottom-most branches to the background (Basics 6).

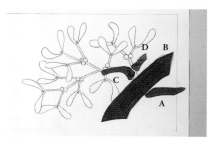

2 Draw the pattern for branches A~D on the front of the fabric pieces and cut them out with a 0.3 cm [⅛"] seam allowance.

3 Place branch A in position and appliqué it down using the tip of the needle to turn the seam allowance under as you go. Refer to Basics 7 to get crisp corners; leave the end open as shown.

4 Turn the seam allowance under and appliqué branch B to the background.

5 Leave the end of branch C open where the berries will overlap, and appliqué down. Then, appliqué branch D, covering any open ends.

6 Appliqué the bottom-most leaves first; followed by those that overlap on top (Basics 8).

7 Appliqué the berries in place and embroider the centers. Embroider little buds between the base of each leaf set.

- January -
Shepherd's Purse

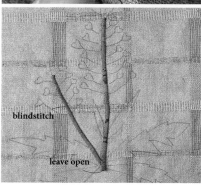

1 Cut the stem from bias strips (Basics 1). Refer to Basics 6 and appliqué the stalks, starting from the one on the left, leaving the end open. Continue to appliqué the center stalk, leaving the end open.

2 Appliqué the berries in place, referring to Basics 9.

3 Appliqué the small leaves (Basics 8).

28

4 Appliqué the large leaves. Begin in a gently curved area and stitch to the tip of the leaf section. In the v-shaped sections, snip into the seam allowance up to 0.2 cm [$^1/_{16}$"] from the mark.

5 Turn the seam allowance at the corner under in 2 steps to create a crisp point (Basics 7). Then continue to appliqué to within 2 stitches of the inner "v".

6 Slide the needle downward and turn the seam allowance under to the position where the snip was made. Take 3 tiny, visible stitches in the "v" to secure. Continue using the same technique around the rest of the leaf. Appliqué the remaining leaves in place.

7 Embroider the stems, flowers and veins in the leaves.

1 Cut the stems from bias strips (Basics 1). Begin to appliqué the shorter stems and trim any excess that extends beyond the width of the long center stem. Next, appliqué the long center stem in place (Basics 6, April - Lotus Flower).

2 Appliqué the leaves (Basics 8). Turn the seam allowance under in 3 steps for a crisp, pointed tip.

 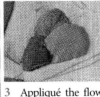

3 Appliqué the flowers and pea pods (Basics 8).

4 Embroider the stems, veins on leaves and peas.

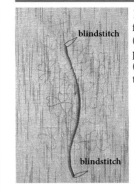

1 Cut the stems from bias strips (Basics 1), and appliqué them down (Basics 6). Stitch all the way around.

2 Appliqué each of the leaves in place (Basics 9).

3 Fill in the flowers with 4 rows of embroidered straight stitches.

4 Embroider the calyxes and stems. Finally, embroider random straight stitches in the middle of the leaves.

Strolling with Greenery

Burnet Handbag

There's a sense of fleeting moments that I wanted to capture when I saw these long, thin branches tipped with subtle red flowers. I kept this vertical flow in mind, wanting to echo the silhouette, when choosing both the fabric and handles for this handbag.
----- instructions p. 66

30

Whether venturing out to walk along a leafy path, or a bustling street, bring your own favorite "greenery" along with you.

Japanese Judas Tree Handbag

I imagined standing under a Judas Tree, looking straight up as I drew this. Young green leaves dappled with sunlight are a soothing sight. I hope you'll try it yourself while out on a walk.

----- instructions p. 68

Angelica Handbag

I love plants where puffy flowers appear at the end of a single stem. For this handbag, sew together six pieces of fabric appliquéd with the same design. I made it appear as though the plants are growing up out of the ground.

----- instructions p. 72

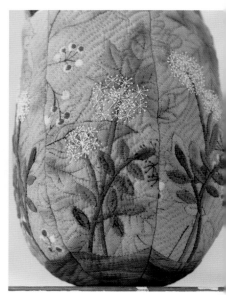

Marguerite Bag

These are the sweetest and most charming
of flowers.   The background fabric is an
ideal backdrop as they gracefully float across
both sides of the bag.

----- instructions p. 74

Dogwood Pouch

On my fabric-buying trips to the United States, I often see dogwood trees. I was fascinated to learn that what we often think of as the flower petals, are actually bracts with color-tipped edges. The slightly-curled edges are delightful.

----- instructions p. 35

34

----- shown on p. 34

Dogwood Pouch

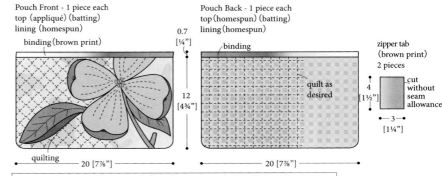

● Dimensional Diagram

Pouch Front - 1 piece each
top (appliqué) (batting)
lining (homespun)
binding (brown print)

Pouch Back - 1 piece each
top (homespun) (batting)
lining (homespun)

binding

quilt as desired

zipper tab
(brown print)
2 pieces

cut without seam allowance

0.7 [¼"]

12 [4¾"]

4 [1½"]

3 [1¼"]

quilting

20 [7⅞"]

20 [7⅞"]

※※ Seam allowances: add a 0.7 cm [¼"] to the top; 0.3 cm [⅛"] to the batting and lining; cut zipper tab without any seam allowance.

✳ Finished Measurements:
   12.7 x 20 cm [5" x 7⅞"]
✳ The full-size template/pattern
   can be found on Side C of the pattern sheet inserts.
✳ Contrasting thread has been used in the photos for
   instructional purposes.

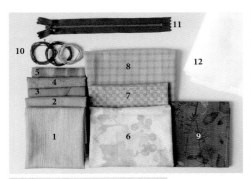

● Materials
1 Dusky pink print - 16 × 16 cm [6¼" × 6¼"]
   (appliqué - petals a, b, c, d)
2 Dusky pink print - scraps (appliqué - petals e, f, g)
3 Lt green print - scraps (appliqué - leaf h)
4 Med green print - 10 × 12 cm [4" × 4¾"](appliqué
   - leaves i, j)
5 Brown print - scraps (appliqué - stems k, l)
6 Lt print - 14 × 22 cm [5½" × 8⅝"](bag front)
7 Homespun - 14 × 22 cm [5½" × 8⅝"](bag back)
8 Homespun - 18 × 52 cm [7⅛" × 20½"](lining)
9 Dk brown print - 3.5 x 45 cm [1⅜" × 17¾"]
   (binding); 4 × 6 cm [1½" × 2⅜"](zipper tab)
10 Embroidery thread - mustard, brown, moss green
11 1 Zipper - 18.5 cm [7¼"](brown)
12 Batting - 18 × 52 cm [7⅛" × 20½"]
13 Waxed cord - 20 cm [7⅞"] (moss green)
14 2 Lg beads - 2.3 cm [⅞"]
15 2 Sm beads - 0.6 cm [¼"]

1 Tracing the Appliqué Design

Cut out the fabric for the front of the bag adding a 0.7 cm [¼"] seam allowance. Trace the appliqué design onto tracing paper by hand (or make a photocopy) and tape it to a light table. Place the fabric for the front of the bag on top of the traced design and center it (tape it in place if desired). Trace the design with a sharp pencil. Do not trace the embroidery lines.

✳ If you don't have a light table, you can tape the design and the fabric securely to a window and transfer the pattern.

2 Making the Appliqué Pattern Pieces

✳ Use a single, fine thread and the blind-stitch when stitching appliqués to any background fabric.

petals

outer petals

leaves

a

b

c

d

e

f

g

j

i

leaf - h

stem

k

l

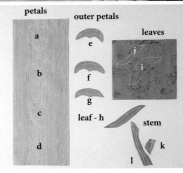

1 Referring to the dimensional diagram and the template/pattern sheet, create individual appliqué pattern templates using thin cardboard or template plastic. Trace the petals a~d on the right side of the fabric. Leave room around each traced petal to allow for the specified seam allowances.※※
Trace leaves i and j on the bias. Trace the outer petals e~g the single leaf h, and stem k and l, leaving a 0.3 cm [⅛"] seam allowance, with the exception of the bottom of stem l, which   should have a 0.5 cm [¼"] seam allowance.

2 Position the outside petal e on top of petal a and pin in place (see left).

3 Take approximately 3 snips into the inner curve of outside petal e.

4 Turn the seam allowance under using the tip of the needle, bringing the needle out approximately 0.3 cm [⅛"] outside of the finished sewing line. Continue to blindstitch all the way to the center point.

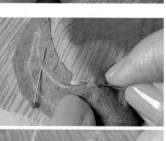

5 Take a few more snips into the second inner curve area and continue to blindstitch to approximately 0.3 cm [⅛"] before the outer point, turning the seam allowance under with the tip of the needle as you go.

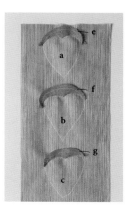

6 Appliqué outer petals f and g to the petals b and c, following steps 2~5 above.

7 Carefully cut out the petals, adding a 0.3 cm [⅛"] seam allowance.

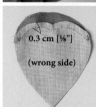

8 Turn the petals over and trim away the extra fabric behind the outer petal appliqué to a 0.3 cm [⅛"] seam allowance.

0.3 cm [⅛"]

(wrong side)

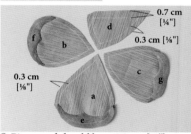

9 Pieces a~d should have 0.3 cm [⅛"] seam allowances, except for the side of piece d that faces the top opening of the bag. Leave a 0.7 cm [¼"] seam allowance as shown above.

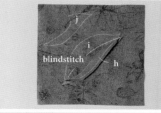

blindstitch

10 Appliqué leaf h onto leaf l, following steps 2~5. Cut leaves i to j, adding a 0.3 cm [⅛"] seam allowance.

3 Appliquéing the Pieces to the Background

leave open

1 Position stem k in place according to the design drawn on the background. Leaving the end open, appliqué around the 3 sides using a blindstitch. Then, position stem l on the background fabric, overlapping the open end of stem k, and pin in place. Appliqué the piece on 3 sides, this time leaving the top open where the flower will overlap the stem (p. 23, Basics 11).

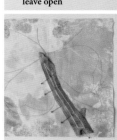

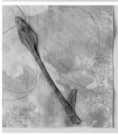

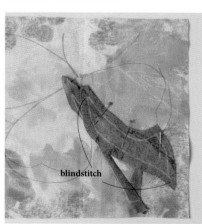

blindstitch

2 Appliqué leaf j in place, snipping into the seam allowance as needed. Stitch up to the tip of the leaf.

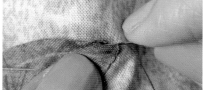

3 Trim the rabbit ear. Turn the seam allowance at the tip of the leaf under in 3 steps, making a crisp corner. Continue to appliqué along the outer edge (p. 22, Basics 7).

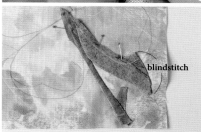

blindstitch

leave open

4 Appliqué leaf i in place, leaving the sides that will be covered by the flower petal open.

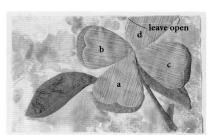

leave open

d

b

c

a

5 Appliqué petals a~d in place, leaving open the outside edge at the top.

4 Adding the Embroidery

✳ Referring to the full-size pattern, lightly draw in the veins in the leaves freehand.
✳ Use an embroidery hoop to keep the fabric taut as you work.
✳ Make a knot on the wrong side of the work before starting; finish off with a knot on the wrong side when finished.

1 The center of the flower is made with french knots. Bring the needle up through the center of the flower, wrap 6 strands of the mustard-colored embroidery thread around the needle 8 times.

in

2 Holding the wrapped threads with your finger, pull the needle all the way through and push it back through close to where you started.

out

3 Bring the needle up again next to the first french knot, and repeat the steps above until you have 8 french knots.

straight stitch

outline stitch

4 Embroider straight stitches in the v-shaped area of the petals; use an outline stitch to make the veins in the leaves.

5 Drawing Quilting Lines

1 Lightly draw lines on the flower petals, using the full-size pattern as a reference. ✳

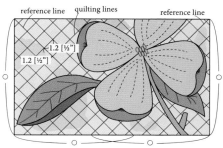

reference line   quilting lines   reference line

1.2 [½"]

1.2 [½"]

2 Draw quilting lines on the background fabric. Quilt as desired, or draw a crosshatch pattern in 1.2 cm [½"] increments.

✳ Use a very sharp soft-lead pencil, and with a light hand, draw thin quilting lines. If the lines are too dark or traced too many times, they can leave residue on the quilting or embroidery thread. If the fabric is dark, use a chalk pencil or marking pen.

6 Basting

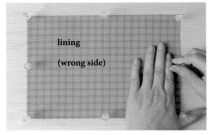

1 Cut the lining (backing) and batting to size referring to the dimensional diagram on p. 35. Smooth the backing fabric out on a flat surface and pin or tape to hold it taut.

2 Lay the batting on top of the lining (backing). Center the appliquéd quilt top on the batting and re-pin or tape all layers to the flat surface.

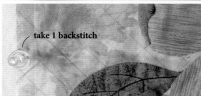

take 1 backstitch

3 Starting in the center of the quilt top with a length of knotted thread, baste all the way to the left edge. Knot the thread at the edge and cut it, leaving a 2-3 cm [¾"~1¼"] tail.

✳ Use a spoon to help lift the needle from the surface as you baste.

4 Start again in the center and baste out to the right edge. Starting in the center, next baste vertically out to the edges on the top and bottom border. Repeat at a diagonal. Finally, baste completely around the edges of the top.

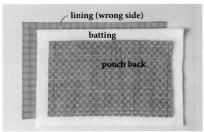

lining (wrong side)

batting

pouch back

5 Refer to steps 1~3 to baste the 3 layers of the pouch back.

7 Quilting

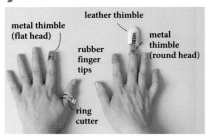

leather thimble

metal thimble (flat head)

metal thimble (round head)

rubber finger tips

ring cutter

1 See the photo for proper finger placement of quilting notions so as not to hurt your fingers while you quilt.

2 Using the non-slip board and weights, place the quilt, as shown, to keep it from moving while you quilt. Always quilt from the center of the quilt toward the outside to minimize puckering.

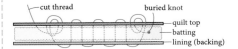

cut thread   buried knot   quilt top   batting   lining (backing)

Beginning the Quilting Stitches

in

out

1 Knot the end of the thread and insert the needle into the quilt top and batting about 2 cm [¾"] away from where you will begin the first stitch. Bring the tip of the needle up and exit at the exact spot for the first stitch without going through the backing.

2 Pull the thread through until the knot is lying on the surface of the quilt top. Gently tug the thread to pop the knot through the quilt top to bury it in the batting.

3 Take another stitch at the exact place where you started. Insert the needle again at the first stitch perpendicular to the top and pull through the back, coming up close to the first stitch.

4 Insert the needle down again until you feel the tip of the needle with your finger under the quilt and come back up. Repeat this rocking motion until you have several stitches on your needle. Then use the thimble to push the needle through the quilt.

1 Bring the needle up in the spot where you want the last stitch to be, leaving a space the width of two stitches in between.

2 Backstitch into the preceding space that was left open, bringing the needle up to create a final stitch. Insert the needle in the last stitch again and work the needle through the batting,

3 Bring up the tip of the needle about 2 cm [¾"] away from the last stitch. Carefully cut the thread close to the quilt top.

Quilting Order

1 Quilt the crosshatching.
2 Quilt lines inside the petals.
3 Outline quilt around each appliqué and add the embroidery.

Outline Quilting

Quilt closely around each appliqué to emphasize their shape.

When the quilting is completed, remove all of the basting stitches except the ones around the edge.

Quilt the pouch back as desired or follow the pattern of the fabric (p. 35, dimensional diagram).

8 Attaching the Binding

Take the full-size template/pattern for the pouch and trace the outline on the lining (backing) side of both the pouch front and back pieces, adding a 0.7 cm [¼"] seam allowance. If the quilting caused some shrinkage of the two pieces, and the pattern will not allow for a 0.7 cm [¼"] seam allowance, it is better to trim the pattern down slightly in order to get the necessary seam allowance.

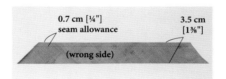

1 Cut 2 bias strips for the top opening of the bag that are 3.5 × 20 cm [1⅜" × 7⅞"] (p. 20, Basics 1).

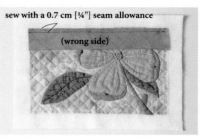

2 With right sides together, match edges of the bias strip and the pouch top and pin in place. Sew from one end to the other with a sewing machine.

3 Trim away the excess batting and the lining (backing) on the top edge.

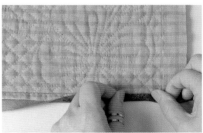

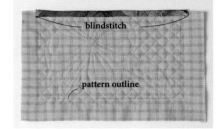

4 Turn the bias strip over to the lining (backing) side and fold in twice to create binding tape; pin in place. Blindstitch the entire length to bind the raw edge.

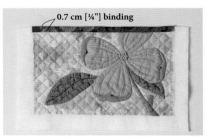

The binding for the pouch front opening is complete.

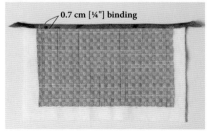

5 Repeat steps 1~4 to bind the pouch back opening.

9 Sewing in the Zipper

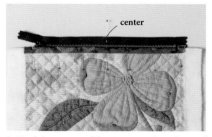

1 Find the center of the zipper and mark it with a pin. Place the zipper behind the pouch front, aligning the centers, and pin in place.

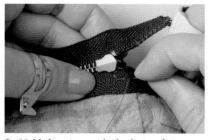

2 Hold the piece with the lining facing you. Starting 0.5 cm [¼"] outside the pattern outline, and using the backstitch, sew the zipper tape (in the middle of the chevron pattern) to the lining, being careful to only catch the batting as you sew. Sew to 0.5 cm [¼"] past the pattern outline.

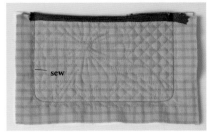

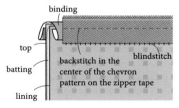

3 Sew down the edge of the zipper tape using a blindstitch, catching the batting in the stitches.

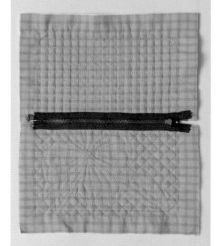

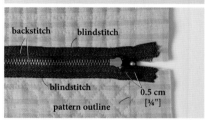

4 Align the pouch back to the zipper and referring to steps 1~3, finish sewing in the zipper.

10 Sewing the Pouch

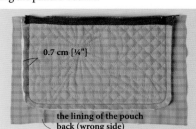

1 Open the zipper most of the way and with right sides together, match the pouch front and back; sew around the sides and bottom following the pattern outline.

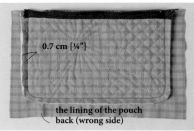

2 Trim all the layers down to a 0.7 cm [¼"] seam allowance, except for the lining (backing) of the pouch back.

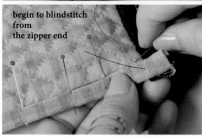

3 Fold the remaining lining (backing) from step 2 over twice to create a binding; pin in place. Starting from the end of the zipper, blindstitch the binding to the lining of the pouch.

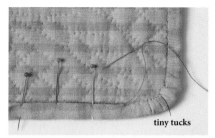

tiny tucks

4 If the remaining lining used to create the inner binding is too wide for the raw edges, trim it down. Take tiny tucks around the corners to ease the fullness. Bind all the way around and up to the beginning of the zipper.

11 Finishing the Zipper

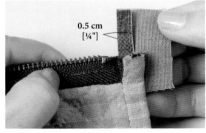

0.5 cm [¼"]

1 Cut out the zipper tab pieces with no seam allowance; turn the long side under 0.5 cm [¼"]. Position the folded edge along the side of the seam.

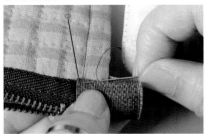

2 Fold the zipper tab over to cover the seam edge. Then fold any excess fabric from the zipper tab under and align it with the edge of the zipper tape and pin. Blindstitch the zipper tab to the bound side seam.

3 Turn the corner and continue to blindstitch across the zipper tape. Take several stitches at the top where the zipper teeth meet and then continue down the opposite side.

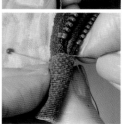

0.5 cm [¼"]

4 In the same way as the other side, fold the excess fabric from the zipper tab under the zipper tape to match the edges. Blindstitch the folded edge of the tab to the bound side seam. Trim off the raw ends of the tab, leaving 0.5 cm [¼"].

5 Fold the 0.5 cm [¼"] seam allowance under and blindstitch the two folded edges together.

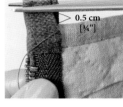

6 Insert the needle close to the last stitch and bring the tip of the needle out at the sewn edge. Pull gently on the thread to round the tip of the fold. Tie a knot close to the fabric; gently pull to pop the knot inside to hide it. Finally, finish the beginning end of the zipper following steps 1~6.

12 Attaching the Zipper Pull

1 Turn the pouch right side out and close the zipper. Using cutting nippers or pliers, cut off the zipper pull.

2 Remove the filament from the center of the waxed cord.

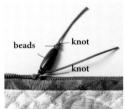

beads   knot

knot

3 Thread the waxed cord through the metal tab on the zipper; fold it in half and tie a knot. String two beads onto the cord and knot it at the end.

4 Leave a 1 cm [⅜"] tail after the knot; cut the cord and feed the tail back through the hole in the beads to secure. Repeat for the second set of beads to finish the zipper pull.

Completed Pouch

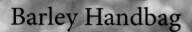

Barley Handbag

Long, slender stalks of barley, ripe with ears of grain and complementary motifs, make up the design of this handbag. The entwined stalks are arranged and appliquéd in ordered layers.

----- instructions p. 76

Peeping Down from Above Handbag

When I look straight down on this plant, I see little, white flowers scattered in the center of flat, wide-spread leaves. When viewed from this angle, it made a lovely design and I couldn't help but make it a focal point on this handbag.

----- instructions p. 78

Sunflower Pouch

The brilliant sunflower is a classic summer flower. I simplified its care-free form, and designed it to fit on this little pouch that can be carried any-where.

----- instructions p. 70

Cow Parsnip Handbag

The flowers of the cow parsnip spread out like little umbrellas. In order to highlight the beauty of the background fabric, I placed the design off-center and focused on the flowers themselves.

----- instructions p. 45

----- shown on p. 44

Cow Parsnip Handbag

✻ Finished Measurements:
  21 × 26 cm [8¼" ×10¼"]; gusset 11 cm [4⅜"]

✻ The full-size template/pattern can be found on
  Side C of the pattern sheet inserts.

✻ Contrasting thread has been used in the photos
  for instructional purposes.

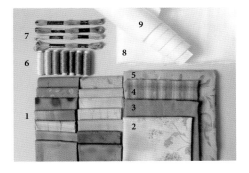

● Materials

1 Assorted fat quarters or scraps (appliqués)
2 Print - 25 × 80 cm [9¾" × 31½"](bag front, bag
   back)
3 Homespun - 40 × 60 cm [15¾" × 23⅝"](handle)
4 Homespun - 14 × 28 cm [5½" × 11"](bottom)
5 Print - 50 × 90 cm [19¾" × 35⅜"] (backing)
6 Fine embroidery thread - 2-strand, colors to
   match fabric
7 Embroidery thread - colors to match fabric
8 Batting - 50 × 90 cm [19¾" × 35⅜"]
9 Fusible interfacing - 22 × 31 cm [8⅝" × 12¼"]

● Dimensional Diagram

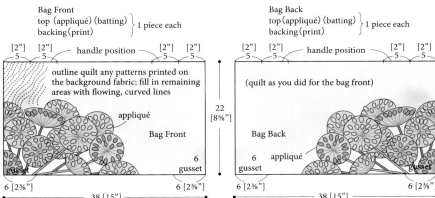

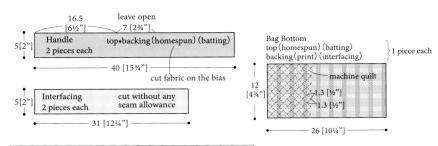

✻✻ Seam allowances: add 3 cm [1¼"] to tops, batting and lining/backing;
1 cm [⅜"] to all other pieces; cut interfacing without any seam allowance.

1 Appliquéing the Front and Back of the Bag

Bag Front

Bag Back

Trace the appliqué pattern for the front of the bag, onto the background fabric and begin to appliqué from the bottom flowers to the top (p. 21, Basics 6). After the appliqué is completed, refer to the pattern and embroider, freehand, the thin stems using an outline stitch.

Reverse the pattern for the bag back to mirror the bag front; appliqué and embroider the bag back, following the same directions as above.

2 Quilting

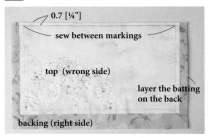

1 With right sides of the bag front and backing together, place the batting against the backing side and machine sew along the top edge between markings. Trim the seam allowance to 0.7 cm [¼"].

2 Turn right side out, folding the seam allowance over to the top side and finger-press the seam (p. 65)

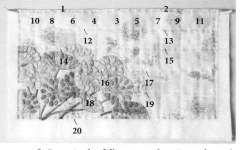

3 Baste in the following order: Baste from the center of the opening to the outside edge (1,2). Baste the center, vertically (3). Working from the inside center line toward the outside edge on either side, baste vertically (4~11). Working from the inside center line toward the outside edge on either side, baste horizontally (12~19). Finally, baste around the outer edge (20).

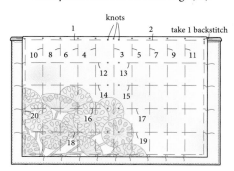

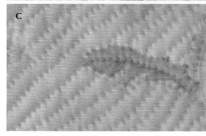

4 Quilt the pieces (p. 38) in the following order: 1) Within each flower, quilt circular lines 0.3-0.4 cm [⅛"] apart (B). 2) Outline quilt any patterns or flowers that are printed on the background fabric. 3) Outline quilt around each of the appliquéd flowers and stems (C). 4) With a marking pencil, draw softly curving freeform lines on the background fabric where there is no quilting (A, C).

Once the quilting is completed, remove all of the basting stitches, except for the stitches around the outer edge.

5 Quilt the back of the bag following step 4.

3 Drawing the bag outline

1 Use straight pins to mark the finished sewing line, 0.7 cm [¼"] in from the side and bottom edges of the bag front.

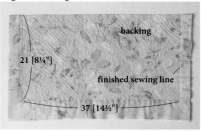

2 Turn the piece over, and with a ruler, draw the side and bottom finished sewing lines, using the pins as a guide. The quilting will have caused the piece to shrink somewhat from the original dimensions.

✳ The shrinkage will depend on the amount of quilting, the fabric used, and the personal quilting style of the quilter. This is expected. Note that the original measurements in the dimensional diagram is a starting place and not intended to match after quilting.

4 Making the bottom

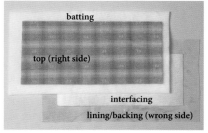

1 Using a marking pencil and ruler, draw the quilting lines on the top fabric (p. 45). Iron the interfacing to the wrong side of the backing fabric. With wrong sides together, layer the top and backing with batting in between.

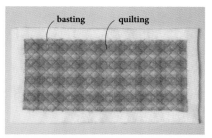

2 Baste the 3 layers, then machine quilt, following the quilting lines. Remove the basting stitches, except for those around the outer edge.

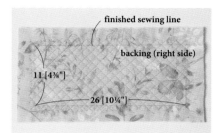

3 With the backing right side up, draw the finished sewing line for the bottom of the bag. This, too, will have some shrinkage due to the quilting. Calculate the size of the bottom by measuring the bottom edge of the bag front/back, less the gusset on each side (and adding 0.7 cm [¼"] for the seam allowance.

5 Constructing the bag

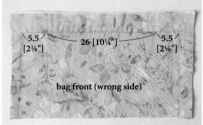

1 With right sides together, place the bottom edges of the front of the bag and the bag bottom together. Align them so that there is a 5.5 cm [2⅛"] (gusset width) on each side of the bag bottom. Pin in place; machine sew along the finished sewing line between the markings.

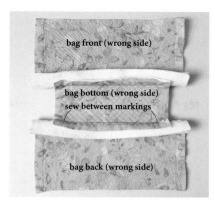

2 Sew the bag bottom to the bag back in the same manner as step 1.

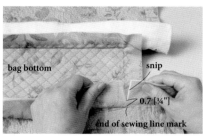

3 Snip the backing and batting down to within 0.7 cm [¼"] of the mark at the end of the finished sewing line. Repeat in all 4 corners.

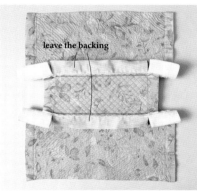

4 Leaving the backing from the bag front and back, trim away the rest of the fabric and batting close to the stitching. Then trim the remaining backing fabric down to a 0.7 cm [¼"] seam allowance to allow for turning under and binding the raw edges.

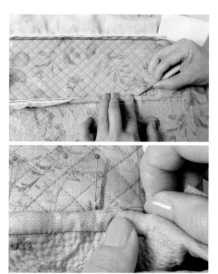

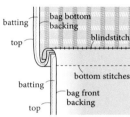

5 Using the trimmed backing fabric, fold it over the raw edges of the seam allowance and lay toward the bottom of the bag; pin in place. Blindstitch down.

6 Finish binding the raw seam allowance on the opposite side of the bag bottom in the same way.

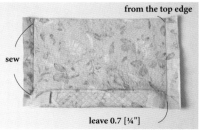

7 Fold the entire piece, right sides together and aligning edges; sew the side seams between markings, leaving 0.7 cm [¼"] unsewn below the bottom mark.

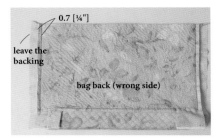

8 Leaving the backing from the bag front and back, trim the rest of the fabric and batting to a 0.7 cm [¼"] seam allowance. Trim the remaining backing fabric to allow for turning under and binding the raw edges of the side seams.

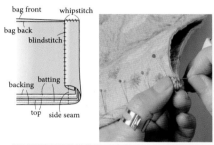

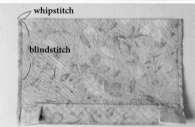

9 Whipstitch the 0.7 cm [¼"] seam allowance at the top edge. Using the trimmed backing fabric, fold it over the raw edges of the side seam and lay toward the bottom of the bag; pin in place. Blindstitch. Repeat for the other side seam.

6 Sewing the Sides

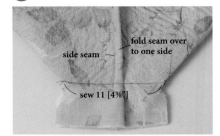

1 Sew the sides and bottom together along the finished sewing lines on both sides.

2 Make 2 bias strips, 2.5 × 13 cm [1" × 5⅛"] (p. 20, Basics 1) out of the same fabric as the backing.

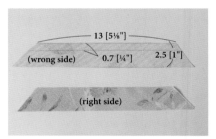

3 With right sides together, align the bias strip with the finished sewing line. Sew from end to end.

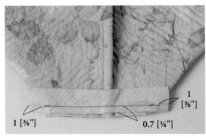

4 Trim away the excess fabric from the bias strip on both ends, leaving a 1 cm [⅜"] seam allowance. Trim the excess bag fabric down to a 0.7 cm [¼"] seam allowance.

5 Fold the bias strip over to bind the raw edge, tucking the 1 cm [⅜"] ends under; pin in place. Blindstitch.

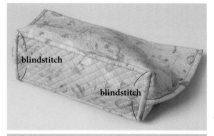

6 Finish the other side of the bag bottom in the same manner. Turn the bag right side out.

7 Making the Handles

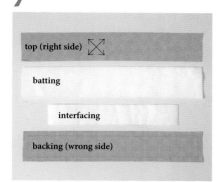

top (right side)

batting

interfacing

backing (wrong side)

1 Refer to p. 45 for the dimensions of each part of the handles.

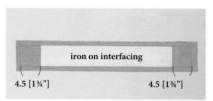

iron on interfacing

4.5 [1¾"]   4.5 [1¾"]

2 Iron the interfacing to the wrong side of the handle backing, centering it.

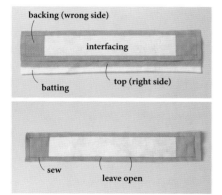

backing (wrong side)

interfacing

batting

top (right side)

sew   leave open

3 With right sides of the handle top and backing together, place the batting against the wrong side of the top fabric and machine sew around the edges, leaving an opening to turn it right side out.

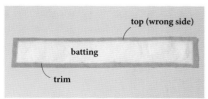

top (wrong side)

batting

trim

4 Trim the batting close to the stitching.

blindstitch closed

5 Turn the handle right side out through the opening; blindstitch it closed. Repeat steps 1~5 to make a second handle.

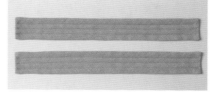

6 Topstitch 3 rows by machine, referring to the diagram on the right.

topstitch

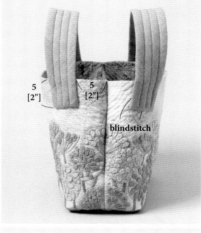

5 [2"]   5 [2"]

blindstitch

7 Place the bag handles 5 cm [2"] down from the top edge, referring to the markings on the pattern. Blindstitch them to the bag, catching the stitching in the batting.

fold the handle in half and sew

fold the handle in half and sandwich the bag fabric; sew

sandwich the bag fabric

8 Fold the handles in half, sandwiching the bag fabric inbetween the two halves. Topstitch along the edges by machine, continuing to topstitch around the entire handle, finishing the same way on the other side. Repeat for the second handle.

Completed Handbag

Oak Leaves & Acorn Bag

A cluster of acorns peek out from the center pleat, surrounded by oak leaves and buds. Choose a background fabric that echoes nature, so that if you quilt the pattern design of the fabric, it almost appears to be appliquéd.
----- instructions p. 80

Horse Chestnut Tote

The large leaves and the chestnuts hidden in their prickly hulls make the horse chestnut a favorite design of mine when working on a plan-inspired theme. This roomy tote is an ideal size and you will want to carry it with you often.

----- instructions p. 82

51

Mountain Ash Bag

The mountain ash, with its distinctive red berries, is depicted in subdued colors. The appliqué is incorporated into the handle to continue the feeling of the swaying branches, while the quilting adds the sense of a gentle breeze.

----- instructions p. 84

Olive Handbag

The oblong fruit and the long leaves of the olive tree are simple shapes that are ideal for appliqué designs. Although somewhat of a complex bag to construct, the subtle colors are soothing and used to perfection in this two-tone handbag.

----- instructions p. 86

Shepherd's Purse Handbag

This little handbag is perfect for a stroll, the appliqué is so life-like that you expect to hear the rustling of the stalks as you walk. The back-side of the handbag has no appliqué and creates a contrasting visual with its circle print and crosshatched quilting.

----- instructions p. 88

Spades & Clubs
Messenger Bag

In a departure from the common plant color palette I've used throughout most of the book, I chose fabric with plaids, checks and dots along with a more modern bag design for a sense of fun and a different feel.

----- instructions p. 90

Fennel Mini Pouch

There was a period of time when I was completely obsessed with herbs. This particular herb is called, "uikyo" in Japanese. Even the name is cute! I designed a small motif to fit within this mini pouch to complement its delicate form.

----- instructions p. 92

Nigella Bag

The first time I saw this flower was as a motif on some stationery. I fell in love with its beauty and it is now one of my favorite flowers. I chose a light background fabric for this piece in order to accentuate the color of the delicate flowers.

----- instructions p. 94

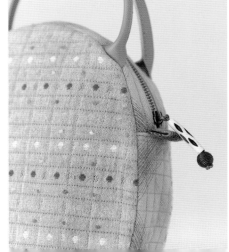

Peas Shopping Bag

It's absolutely delightful, the way that peas sprout so quickly! I left the batting out of this bag. It's a unique shape with looped handles that can easily fold up to carry with you, which is handy. The off-center panels of the background also make this design unusual and interesting.

----- instructions p. 96

Wild Strawberry Shoulder Bag

Seeing wild strawberries always reminds me of the coming of spring. The muted colors of the bag contrast nicely with the vibrant red of the berries and the bright white of the flowers. The tiny, serrated edges of the leaves are created with embroidery stitches.

----- instructions p. 98

The Quilted Woods

After strolling along paths of green, we find our-selves in the woods with the trees and plants all around us. Using the seasonal plants we've dis-covered on our walks, let's bring the designs together into a wall quilt full of greenery.

The Tale of Twelve Plants

Twelve different designs, from the "Plants through the Four Seasons", are appliquéd onto the background that makes the quilt. The quilting within each panel is uniquely different, with soft lines rippling around the border. Use the patterns in the fabric to enhance the quilting.

----- instructions p. 110

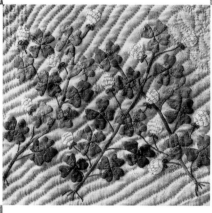

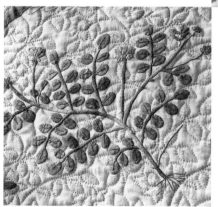

"Woods of Green" Wall Quilt

All 24 designs, chosen to display their individual beauty and characteristics in this wall quilt, are shown between two sturdy tree trunks and the woodland floor. Each block is framed with embroidery to soften the seams. Quilt softly-curving lines in the border and through the trees to give the impression of the wind blowing gently through the trees.

----- instructions p. 100

Essential Quilting Notions & Tools

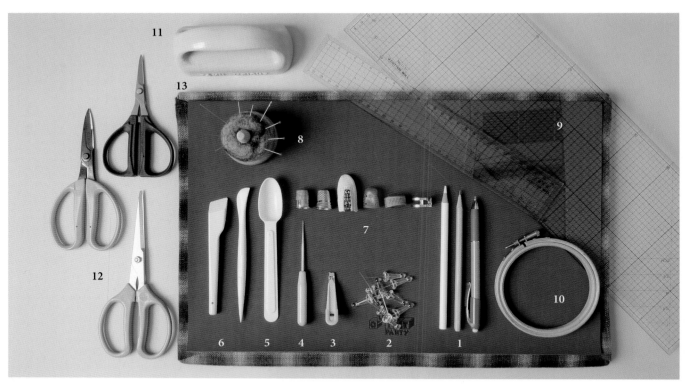

1. Pencils • Colored Pencils • Chalk Pencils
[Pencils] Used for copying patterns, or marking quilting lines. If you use a pencil to mark quilting lines, use one with soft lead. [Colored Pencils] Used for marking the wrong side of fabric. The lines won't always disappear, so do not use for marking quilting lines. • [Chalk Pencils] Used to make marks on fabric where pencil lines won't show up well.

2. Push Pins
Useful to keep layers from shifting when getting ready to baste quilting sandwich. The longer the pin, the better.

3. Bias Tape Maker
Used to guide bias strips through as you iron to make binding.

4. Awl
To mark points when transferring and drawing patterns.

5. Spoon
Often used when pin basting a quilt. Safety pins are easy to use for this method.

6. Seam Pressing Tools
Used to press seam allowances down in lieu of ironing when working with appliqué pieces. (Finger Presser, Hera Markers).

7. Thimbles (from left to right)
[Metal Thimble] Used to push needle through cloth when quilting. (Flat and Round Head) [Leather Thimble] slip this over a metal thimble on your middle finger as you work to keep work from slipping. [Rubber Finger Tips] Wear on your right index finger during quilting or appliqué to help grab the needle and reduce slippage. [Ring Cutter] Conveniently worn on your left (or right) thumb and used for cutting threads as you are working. [Adjustable Thimble] Used when piecing by hand.

8. Pins & Needles
Appliqué Needles, quilting betweens, basting needles, embroidery needles, sewing needles, appliqué pins (small heads, short pins), pins

9. Rulers
Used to trace straight lines when transferring patterns. Rulers with markings made for quilters are useful.

10. Embroidery Hoop
To hold fabric while doing fine embroidery stitches.

11. Weights (paperweights, beanbags, etc.)
Used to weigh down a small quilt when quilting.

12. Scissors
They will last longer if used for specific things, such as for paper, fabric or thread.

13. Non-Slip Board
The non-slip surface board is used when marking fabric or when using the fabric pressing tool to turn under the seam allowances. The soft side backed with batting and fabric can be used as a mini ironing surface.

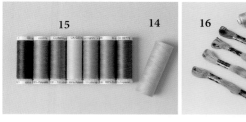

14. Basting Thread
Used for basting.

15. Thread
Used for piecing, stitching, quilting and machine sewing. Use shades of thread that closely match the fabric color.

16. Embroidery Thread/Floss (Easily separated into strands of two)
Used for embroidery.

* **Other notions and tools might be necessary:**
Hoops (quilting), quilt stand (used when quilting large projects), heavy-weight paper (for templates/patterns), tracing paper, light table, cellophane tape, iron, spray adhesive.

Project Instructions (for projects shown on p. 30-62)

Before You Begin

▶ All measurements listed for the following projects are in centimeters (cm) and in inches [in brackets].

▶ The dimensions of the finished project are listed for each, as well as shown in the drawings. Note that the quilted pieces tend to shrink somewhat, depending on the type of fabric used, the thickness of the batting, the amount of quilting and individual quilting technique.

▶ Typically, both the sewing and quilting thread should be the same color as the fabric you are working with. However, use a beige-colored thread if you wish the quilting to stand out.

▶ While most of the work in the projects is done by hand, I do sew the bags together by sewing machine. If you choose to hand-stitch them, make sure to use a backstitch for strength.

Quilting Terminology

Piece - shaped pieces of fabric that will be stitched together; often triangular, square and diamond-shapes.
Piecing - sewing fabric pieces (triangles, squares, etc.) together to create segments or blocks for a quilt top.
Blocks - units that are made up of piecing. Typically, a number of similar blocks sewn together create a quilt top.
Patterns - a design created by sewing fabric pieces or appliqués together.
Sashing - fabric strips that are sewn between blocks.
Borders - strip(s) of fabric that frame the edge of the quilt.
Quilting lines - lines drawn on the fabric to assist in quilting patterns.

Quilting - enclosing a warm layer of batting between two layers of fabric and kept in place by lines of stitching.
Outline quilting - quilting right next to seam lines or appliqués to highlight the designs.
Pressing seams - in quilting, this refers to pressing the seam allowances to one side (usually toward the darker fabric). When pressing hand-pieced seams, leave 0.1 cm [$^1/_{16}$"] showing over the fold to hide the seam and press.
Binding - covering raw edges with a folded and stitched-down width of fabric on both the front and back. Most often made of bias fabric.

Basic Hand-Sewing Stitches and Methods

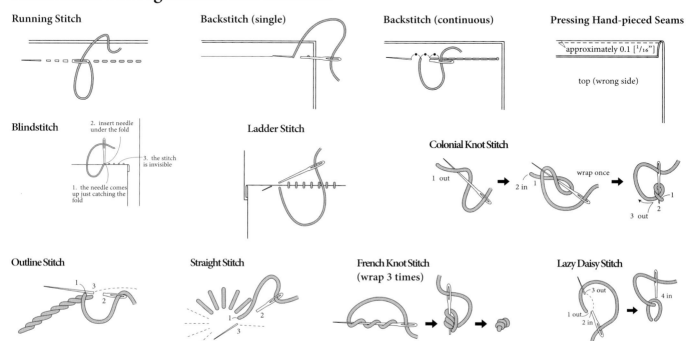

Running Stitch

Backstitch (single)

Backstitch (continuous)

Pressing Hand-pieced Seams
approximately 0.1 [$^1/_{16}$"]
top (wrong side)

Blindstitch
2. insert needle under the fold
3. the stitch is invisible
1. the needle comes up just catching the fold

Ladder Stitch

Colonial Knot Stitch
1 out
2 in
wrap once
1
2
3 out

Outline Stitch
1
3
2

Straight Stitch
1
2
3

French Knot Stitch (wrap 3 times)

Lazy Daisy Stitch
3 out
4 in
1 out
2 in

----- shown on p. 30

Burnet Handbag

∗ Finished Measurements:
   35 × 41 cm [13¾" × 16⅛"]
∗ The full-size template/pattern can be found on Side C of the
   pattern sheet inserts.

● Materials

Cottons
   Brown print - 110 × 40 cm [43¼" × 15¾"] (top)
   Dk green print - 110 × 42 cm [43¼" × 16½"] (backing, handle facing)
   Dk red print - fat quarter or scraps (buds appliqué)
   Beige print - fat quarter or scraps (buds appliqué)
   Pale green print - fat quarter or scraps (leaf appliqué)
   Dk brown print - 2 fat quarters or scraps (bias strips for stems)
Flannel - 110 × 42 cm [43¼" × 16½"]
Faux leather handles - 1 pair

● Instructions

1 Cut out each of the bag pieces referring to the template/pattern and dimensional diagram. Trace the appliqué design directly onto both the top front and top back of the bag using a marking pencil.

2 Trace and cut out the appliqué patterns, adding specified seam allowance∗. Appliqué the flowers, leaves and stems to both sides of the bag.

3 Lay the top fabric and backing with right sides together; layer the flannel next to the wrong side of the backing and machine sew the top opening between markings (Fig. 1). Trim the seam allowance down to 0.7 cm [¼"] and turn right side out; press.

4 Referring to Fig. 2, baste the layers together. Either draw, or freehand quilt, curved, flowing quilting lines (0.7 cm [¼"] apart) on the diagonal . Start in one corner of the bag and work your way to the opposite corner. Repeat steps 3~4 for the back of the bag.

5 As the pieces will have likely shrunk somewhat from the quilting, place the bag pattern on the backing side and re-draw the outline. Mark the lines for making the tucks, starting in the middle and working out to either side. Make the tucks; pin them in place, then machine sew them (Fig. 3).

6 Match the front and back of the bag with right sides together and sew across the sides and bottom (Fig. 4). Bind the inner raw seam allowances referring to Fig. 5.

7 Sew the handles in place on the inside of the bag and make the facing pieces to cover the handle ends. Blindstitch the facings in place (Fig. 6).

● Dimensional Diagram

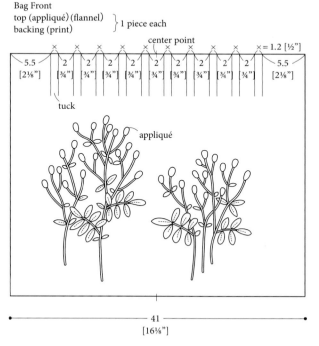

Bag Front
top (appliqué) (flannel) } 1 piece each
backing (print)

center point

× = 1.2 [½"]

5.5 [2⅛"] 2 [¾"] 2 [¾"] 2 [¾"] 2 [¾"] 2 [¾"] 2 [¾"] 2 [¾"] 2 [¾"] 2 [¾"] 5.5 [2⅛"]

tuck

appliqué

35 [13¾"]

41 [16⅛"]

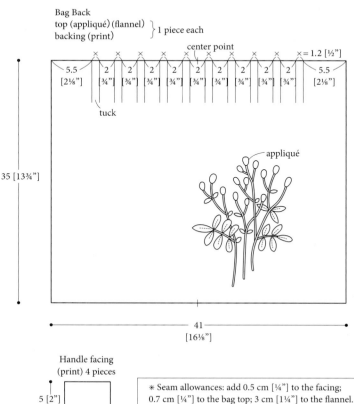

Bag Back
top (appliqué) (flannel) } 1 piece each
backing (print)

center point

× = 1.2 [½"]

5.5 [2⅛"] 2 [¾"] 2 [¾"] 2 [¾"] 2 [¾"] 2 [¾"] 2 [¾"] 2 [¾"] 2 [¾"] 2 [¾"] 5.5 [2⅛"]

tuck

appliqué

41 [16⅛"]

Handle facing
(print) 4 pieces

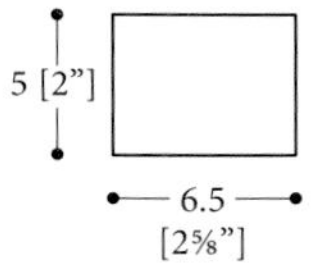

5 [2"]

6.5 [2⅝"]

∗ Seam allowances: add 0.5 cm [¼"] to the facing;
0.7 cm [¼"] to the bag top; 3 cm [1¼"] to the flannel.

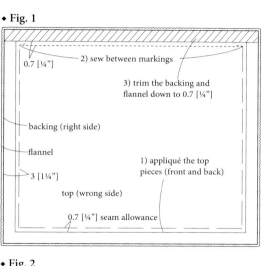

◆ Fig. 1

2) sew between markings

0.7 [¼"]

3) trim the backing and flannel down to 0.7 [¼"]

backing (right side)

flannel

3 [1¼"]

1) appliqué the top pieces (front and back)

top (wrong side)

0.7 [¼"] seam allowance

◆ Fig. 2

3) quilt curved, flowing lines

1) press the seam allowance toward the top

backing

flannel

top

2) baste (p. 46)

4) remove all basting stitches except around the edges after quilting

quilt around each appliqué

◆ Fig. 4

bag back

bag front

3) trim the top and flannel seam allowance down to 0.7 [¼"]; leave the backing and use to bind the raw edges

1) sew the sides and bottom seams with right sides together

2) trim the backing and flannel seam allowance down to 0.7 [¼"]; leave the top to use to bind the raw edges

◆ Fig. 5

Binding the inner side seams

flannel

top

flannel

backing

bag back

side seam

using the backing fabric, fold over the raw seam allowances toward the bag front and blindstitch down

Binding the inner bottom seam

using the top fabric, fold over the raw seam allowances toward the bag front and blindstitch down

top

flannel

backing of bag back

bottom seam

handle (right side)

1 [⅜"]

[2⅜"] 6

center point

3 [1¼"]

backstitch at the beginning and end to secure stitching

5.5 [2⅛"]

1 [⅜"]

[½"] 1.2 [½"] 1.2 [½"] 1.2 [½"] 1.2 [½"] 1.2

2 [¾"] 2 [¾"] 2 [¾"] 2 [¾"] 2 [¾"]

6 [2⅜"]

tuck

[¾"] 2

center point

make 5 tucks on each sides of the center point

6 [2⅜"] 0.6 [¼"]

top (right side)

◆ Fig. 6

handle (right side)

(wrong side)

5.5 [2⅛"]

facing

6.5 [2⅜"]

press the seam allowance under on all sides to hide the handle; blind-stitch all around

◆ Fig. 3

make tucks at the top opening

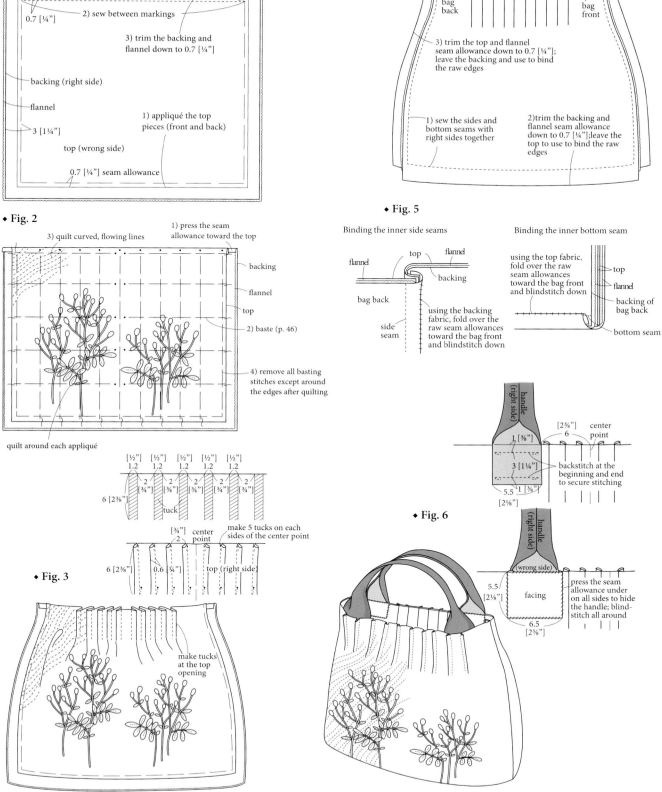

67

----- shown on p. 31

Japanese Judas Tree Handbag

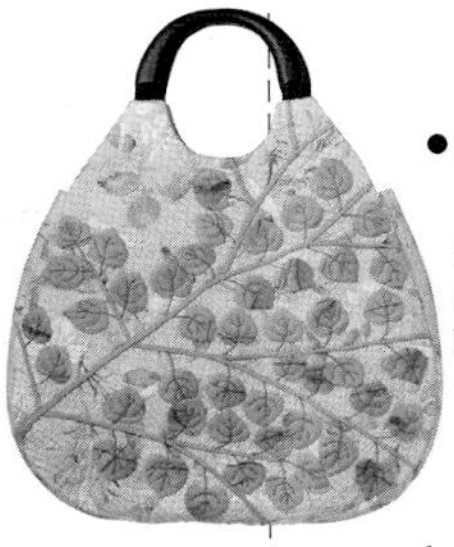

∗ Finished Measurements:
35 × 33 cm [13¾" × 13"]; 6 cm [2⅜"] gusset
∗ The full-size template/pattern can be found on Side B of the pattern sheet inserts.

• Materials

Cottons
- Beige print - 110 × 65 cm [43¼" × 25⅝"] (bag top - front and back, gusset top)
- Beige homespun - 110 × 55 cm [43¼" × 21⅝"] (bag backing, gusset backing, facing, pocket)
- Dk brown print - 8 × 40 cm [3⅛" × 15¾"] (handle loops)
- Beige print - fat quarter or scraps (buds appliqué)
- Pale green print - fat quarter or scraps (leaf appliqué)
- Pale green print - 1.2 cm [½"] bias strips (for stems)

Batting - 90 × 55 cm [35⅜" × 21⅝"]
Fusible interfacing (heavyweight) - 20 × 80 cm [7⅞" × 31½"]
Fusible interfacing (lightweight) - 6 × 12 cm [2⅜" × 4¾"]
Embroidery thread - pale olive
Handles - 1 pair

• Instructions

1 Cut out each of the bag pieces referring to the template/pattern and dimensional diagram. Trace the appliqué design directly onto both the top front and top back of the bag using a marking pencil, reversing the design horizontally on the top back.
2 Trace and cut out the appliqué patterns, adding specified seam allowance*. Appliqué the leaves and branches to both sides of the bag; embroider the veins on the leaves referring to the design (Fig. 1).
3 With wrong sides together, layer the top and backing with the batting in between; baste. Quilt as shown (Fig. 1) or desired. Once the quilting is completed, remove all of the basting stitches, except for those around the outer edge. Baste and quilt the bag back in the same manner. Trace the outline of the bag pattern on the backing of both the bag front and bag back.
4 Refer to Fig. 2 to make the gusset.
5 Iron the heavyweight interfacing to the wrong side of the facing fabric, and fold the seam allowance from the bottom edge up; press (Fig. 3). Make 2.
6 Pin the facing and gusset to the bag front with right sides together, matching edges and markings; sew between the markings at the top and around the edges of the bag (Fig. 4). Repeat for the bag back.
7 Trim the top and batting down to a 0.7 cm [¼"] seam allowance for the gusset, leaving the backing fabric. Then, folding over the backing fabric, bind the raw edges and blindstitch down on both the bag front and back (Fig. 5).
8 Make the handle loop referring to Fig. 6 (p. 86, 87). Insert loop through the handle and sandwich between the bag and the facing (Fig. 7) with the raw edges pulled through the openings in the top of the bag between markings. Stitch across the openings to secure the handle loops.
9 Refer to Fig. 8 to make the inside pocket. Then, turn the facing on both the bag front and back right side out. Place the inside pocket with the upper section tucked under the facing; blindstitch the pocket to the facing, catching the batting (Fig. 9).
10 Blindstitch the bottom edge of the facing to the backing of the bag. Turn the bag right side out to complete.

• Dimensional Diagram

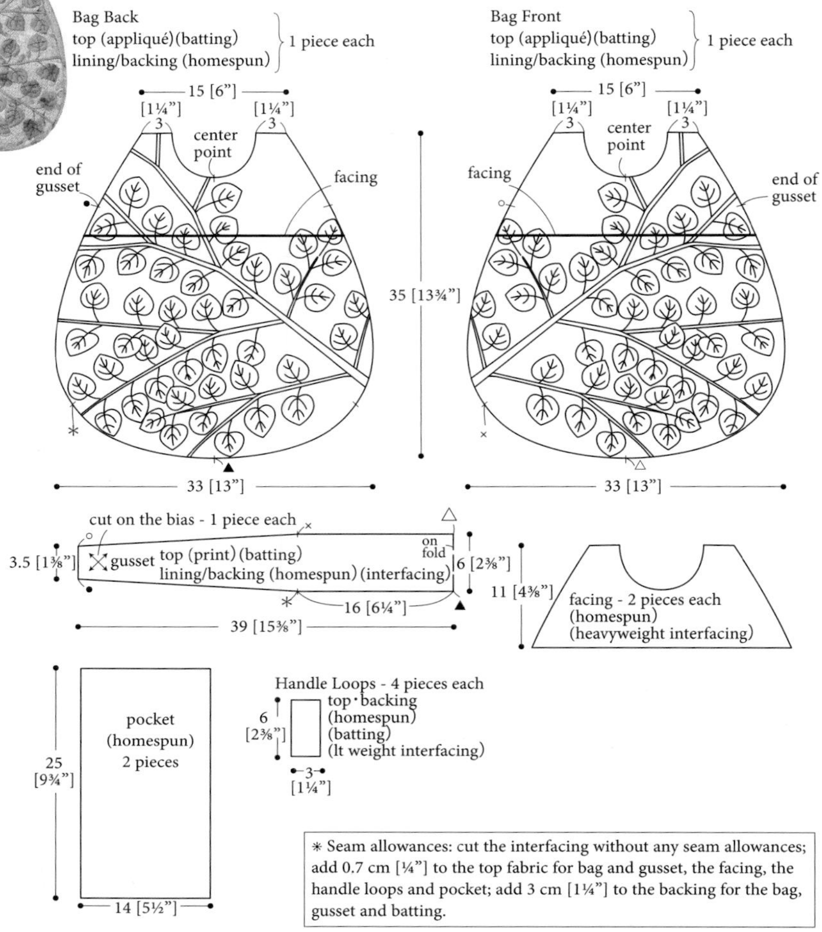
Bag Back
top (appliqué)(batting)
lining/backing (homespun)
1 piece each
15 [6"]
[1¼"] 3
[1¼"] 3
center point
end of gusset
facing
35 [13¾"]
33 [13"]
Bag Front
top (appliqué)(batting)
lining/backing (homespun)
1 piece each
15 [6"]
[1¼"] 3
[1¼"] 3
center point
facing
end of gusset
33 [13"]
cut on the bias - 1 piece each
3.5 [1⅜"]
gusset
top (print) (batting)
lining/backing (homespun) (interfacing)
on fold
6 [2⅜"]
16 [6¼"]
39 [15⅜"]
11 [4⅜"]
facing - 2 pieces each
(homespun)
(heavyweight interfacing)
25 [9¾"]
pocket
(homespun)
2 pieces
14 [5½"]
Handle Loops - 4 pieces each
6 [2⅜"]
top · backing
(homespun)
(batting)
(lt weight interfacing)
3 [1¼"]

∗ Seam allowances: cut the interfacing without any seam allowances; add 0.7 cm [¼"] to the top fabric for bag and gusset, the facing, the handle loops and pocket; add 3 cm [1¼"] to the backing for the bag, gusset and batting.

◆ **Fig. 1**

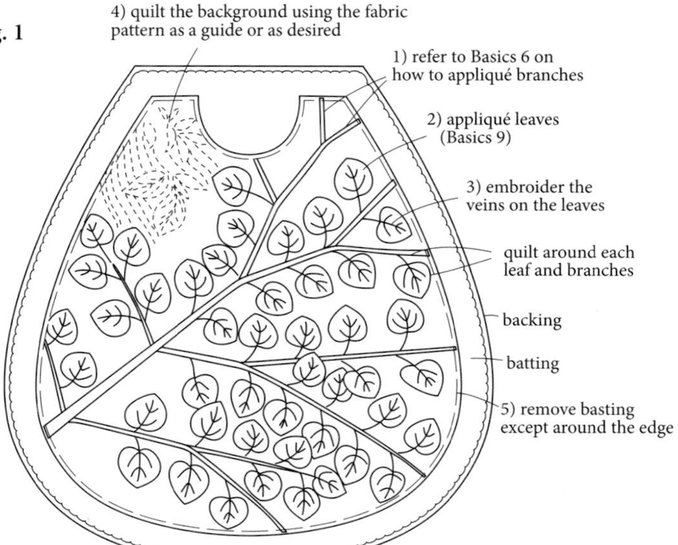
4) quilt the background using the fabric pattern as a guide or as desired
1) refer to Basics 6 on how to appliqué branches
2) appliqué leaves (Basics 9)
3) embroider the veins on the leaves
quilt around each leaf and branches
backing
batting
5) remove basting except around the edge

◆ Fig. 2

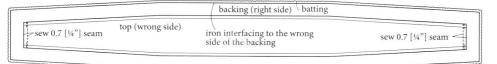

backing (right side) · batting

top (wrong side)   iron interfacing to the wrong
sew 0.7 [¼"] seam   side of the backing   sew 0.7 [¼"] seam

1) lay the gusset top and gusset backing with right sides together; place the batting
on top of the wrong side of the backing; sew both ends

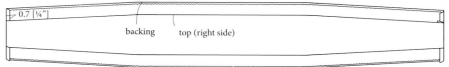

0.7 [¼"]

backing   top (right side)

2) trim the sewn gusset ends backing fabric down to 0.7 [¼"]; trim the batting close to
the stitching; turn right side out

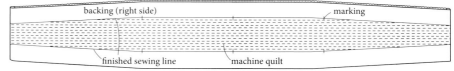

backing (right side)   marking

finished sewing line   machine quilt

3) machine quilt parallel lines as shown, or quilt as desired; draw the
finished sewing line on the backing with a marking pencil

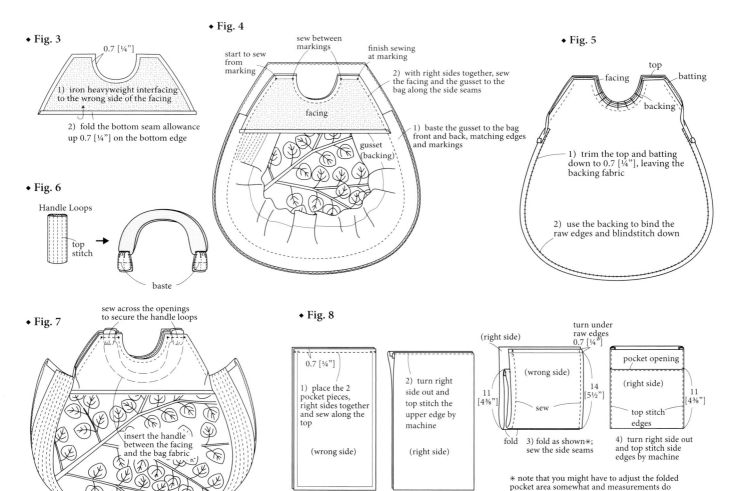

◆ Fig. 3

0.7 [¼"]

1) iron heavyweight interfacing
to the wrong side of the facing

2) fold the bottom seam allowance
up 0.7 [¼"] on the bottom edge

◆ Fig. 6

Handle Loops

top
stitch

baste

◆ Fig. 4

sew between
markings

start to sew
from
marking

finish sewing
at marking

facing

gusset
(backing)

2) with right sides together, sew
the facing and the gusset to the
bag along the side seams

1) baste the gusset to the bag
front and back, matching edges
and markings

◆ Fig. 5

top

facing   batting

backing

1) trim the top and batting
down to 0.7 [¼"], leaving the
backing fabric

2) use the backing to bind the
raw edges and blindstitch down

◆ Fig. 7

sew across the openings
to secure the handle loops

insert the handle
between the facing
and the bag fabric

◆ Fig. 8

0.7 [¼"]

1) place the 2
pocket pieces,
right sides together
and sew along the
top

(wrong side)

2) turn right
side out and
top stitch the
upper edge by
machine

(right side)

(right side)

turn under
raw edges
0.7 [¼"]

(wrong side)

11
[4⅜"]   14
                 [5½"]

sew

fold

3) fold as shown*;
sew the side seams

pocket opening

(right side)

11
[4⅜"]

top stitch
edges

4) turn right side out
and top stitch side
edges by machine

* note that you might have to adjust the folded
pocket area somewhat and measurements do
not have to be exact.

69

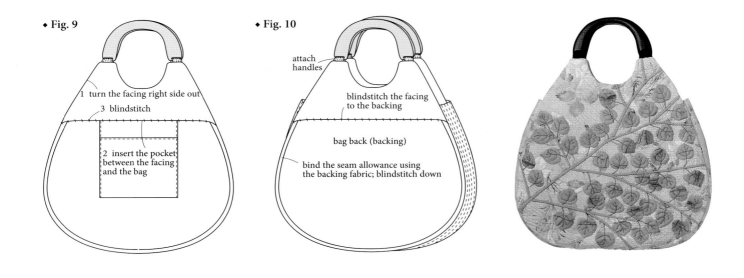

◆ Fig. 9

1 turn the facing right side out

3 blindstitch

2 insert the pocket between the facing and the bag

◆ Fig. 10

attach handles

blindstitch the facing to the backing

bag back (backing)

bind the seam allowance using the backing fabric; blindstitch down

----- shown on p. 43

Sunflower Pouch

❋ Finished Measurements:
17 × 10 cm [6¾" × 4"]; 3 cm [1¼"] gusset
❋ The full-size template/pattern can be found on Side C of the pattern sheet inserts.

● Materials
Cottons
    Brown homespun - 19 × 12 cm [7½" × 4¾"] (front top)
    Beige homespun - 19 × 12 cm [7½" × 4¾"] (back top)
    Grey homespun - 32 × 5 cm [12⅝" × 2"] (gusset top)
    Green homespun - 25 × 35 cm [9¾" × 13¾"] (backing)
    Brown homespun - 20 × 4 cm [7⅞" × 1½"] (strap backing)
    Fat quarter or scraps (appliqué, strap top, strap end)
Batting - 50 × 30 cm [19¾" × 11¾"]
Fusible interfacing - 19 × 2 cm [7½" × ¾"]
Waxed cord (black) - 2 cm [¾"]
Embroidery thread - dk brown
Purse clasp - 1 set
Metal O-ring (small)

● Instructions

1 Cut out each of the pouch pieces referring to the template/pattern and dimensional diagram. Trace the appliqué design directly onto the top front of the pouch using a marking pencil. Trace and cut out the appliqué patterns, adding specified seam allowance*. Appliqué to the front of the bag.
2 With right sides together, layer the top and backing with the batting next to the backing; sew around the edges, leaving an opening (Fig. 1). Trim the batting close to stitching; turn right side out through opening. Press and quilt as shown (Fig. 2) or desired.
3 Make the pouch back using the same method as the pouch front, without the appliqué, and quilt as shown (Fig. 3).
4 Refer to Fig. 4 to make the gusset. With right sides together, sew the bag top and back to the gusset using a whipstitch (Fig. 5).
5 Refer to Fig. 6 to attach the purse clasp to the top of the pouch front and back using a backstitch.
6 Refer to Fig. 7 to make the strap, attach the strap end and waxed cord loop.
7 Attach the O-ring to the metal clasp and the strap (Fig. 8).

● Dimensional Diagram

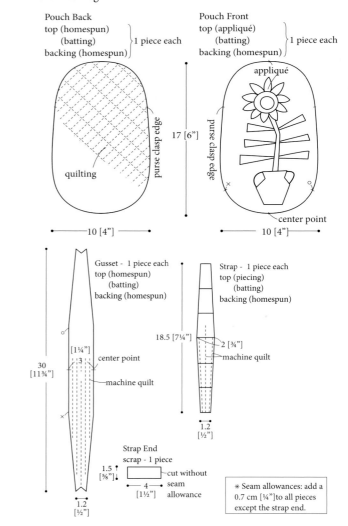

Pouch Back
top (homespun)
(batting)
backing (homespun)
1 piece each

quilting

purse clasp edge

Pouch Front
top (appliqué)
(batting)
backing (homespun)
1 piece each

appliqué

purse clasp edge

17 [6"]

center point

10 [4"]

10 [4"]

Gusset - 1 piece each
top (homespun)
(batting)
backing (homespun)

[1¼"]
3
center point

machine quilt

30 [11¾"]

1.2 [½"]

Strap - 1 piece each
top (piecing)
(batting)
backing (homespun)

18.5 [7¼"]

2 [¾"]
machine quilt

1.2 [½"]

Strap End
scrap - 1 piece

cut without seam allowance

1.5 [⅝"]

4 [1½"]

❋ Seam allowances: add a 0.7 cm [¼"] to all pieces except the strap end.

70

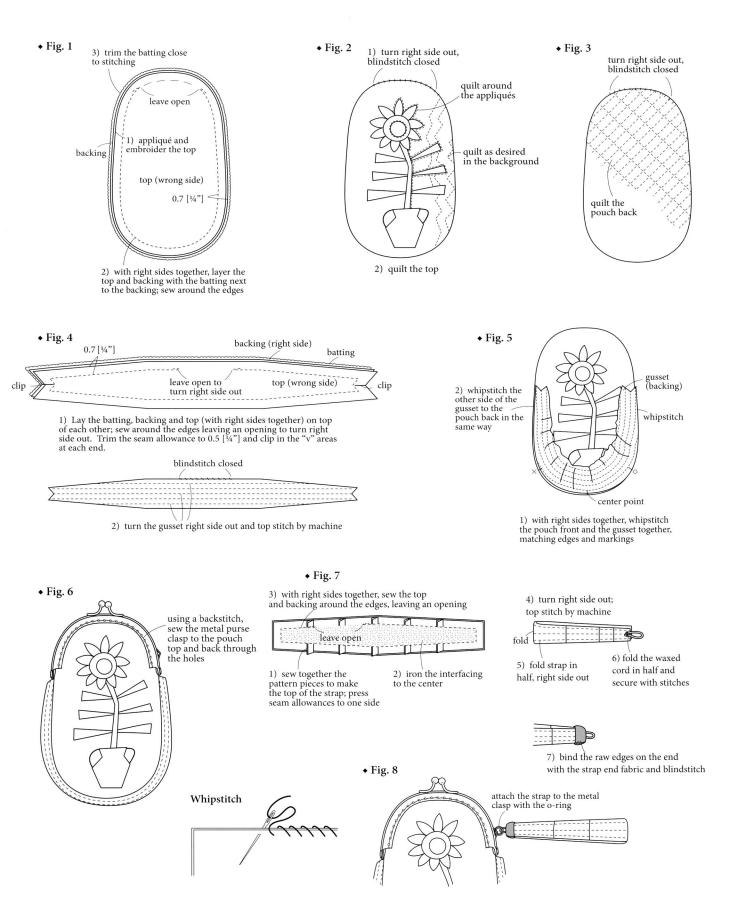

♦ **Fig. 1**

3) trim the batting close to stitching

leave open

1) appliqué and embroider the top

backing

top (wrong side)

0.7 [¼"]

2) with right sides together, layer the top and backing with the batting next to the backing; sew around the edges

♦ **Fig. 2**

1) turn right side out, blindstitch closed

quilt around the appliqués

quilt as desired in the background

2) quilt the top

♦ **Fig. 3**

turn right side out, blindstitch closed

quilt the pouch back

♦ **Fig. 4**

0.7 [¼"]

backing (right side)

batting

clip

leave open to turn right side out

top (wrong side)

clip

1) Lay the batting, backing and top (with right sides together) on top of each other; sew around the edges leaving an opening to turn right side out. Trim the seam allowance to 0.5 [¼"] and clip in the "v" areas at each end.

blindstitch closed

2) turn the gusset right side out and top stitch by machine

♦ **Fig. 5**

2) whipstitch the other side of the gusset to the pouch back in the same way

gusset (backing)

whipstitch

center point

1) with right sides together, whipstitch the pouch front and the gusset together, matching edges and markings

♦ **Fig. 6**

using a backstitch, sew the metal purse clasp to the pouch top and back through the holes

♦ **Fig. 7**

3) with right sides together, sew the top and backing around the edges, leaving an opening

leave open

1) sew together the pattern pieces to make the top of the strap; press seam allowances to one side

2) iron the interfacing to the center

4) turn right side out; top stitch by machine

fold

5) fold strap in half, right side out

6) fold the waxed cord in half and secure with stitches

7) bind the raw edges on the end with the strap end fabric and blindstitch

♦ **Fig. 8**

attach the strap to the metal clasp with the o-ring

Whipstitch

----- shown on p. 32

Angelica Handbag

✻ Finished Measurements:
34 [13⅜"]; 16 cm [6¼"] at the opening
✻ The full-size template/pattern can be found on Side C of the pattern sheet inserts.

● Materials

Cottons
    2 Grey prints - 55 × 32 cm [21⅝" × 12⅝"] (top and lining - 1 grey each)
    Brown print - 60 × 10 cm [23⅝" × 4"] (appliqué for bottom)
    Green prints - fat quarter or scrap (leaf appliqué, bias strips for stems)
    Pale green prints - fat quarter or scrap (leaf appliqué)
    Beige print - 100 × 5 cm [39⅜" × 2"] (scalloped edging)
    Grey homespun - 20 × 65 cm [7⅞" × 25⅝"] (handle)
    Muslin - 110 × 32 cm [43¼" × 12⅝"] (facing)
Batting - 90 × 30 cm [35⅜" × 11¾"]
Flannel - 55 × 5 cm [21⅝" × 2"]
Fusible batting - 20 × 65 cm [7⅞" × 25⅝"]
Fusible interfacing (lightweight) - 10 × 65 cm [4" × 25⅝"]
Embroidery thread - lt beige
Spray adhesive

● Dimensional Diagram

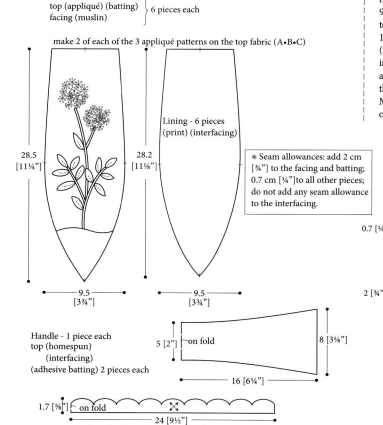

Bag
top (appliqué) (batting) } 6 pieces each
facing (muslin)

make 2 of each of the 3 appliqué patterns on the top fabric (A•B•C)

28.5 [11¼"]

28.2 [11⅛"]

Lining - 6 pieces (print) (interfacing)

9.5 [3¾"]

9.5 [3¾"]

✻ Seam allowances: add 2 cm [¾"] to the facing and batting; 0.7 cm [¼"] to all other pieces; do not add any seam allowance to the interfacing.

Handle - 1 piece each
top (homespun)
(interfacing)
(adhesive batting) 2 pieces each

5 [2"] on fold

8 [3⅛"]

16 [6¼"]

1.7 [⅝"] on fold

24 [9½"]

Scalloped Edge
top (print) - 2 pieces each
flannel - 1 piece

● Instructions

1 Cut out each of the bag pieces referring to the template/pattern and dimensional diagram. Trace the appliqué design directly onto the 6 pieces (2 each of A•B•C) of the top front of the bag using a marking pencil. Trace and cut out the appliqué patterns, adding specified seam allowance✻. Appliqué the stems and leaves to the 6 top pieces; embroider the flowers, referring to the pattern.

2 Layer the top and facing, wrong sides together, with the batting in between; baste. Quilt as shown, or as desired (Fig. 1). Repeat for all 6 pieces.

3 With right sides together, sew A and B between markings along the sides, from bottom to top. With right sides together, sew C to the other side of B. Trim the seam allowances down to 0.7 cm [¼"] and press the seams open. Make a second set (Fig. 2).

4 With right sides together, match the edges and seams of the first set to the second set; pin in place and sew them together to create the outer bag (Fig. 3). Trim the seam allowances down to 0.7 cm [¼"] and press the seams open.

5 Cut 2 bias strips to make the scalloped edge. Place them, right sides together, on top of the flannel. Sew around the ends and the scallops, leaving the bottom edge open. Trim the flannel down to 0.7 cm [¼"]; snip in the "v" of each scallop and turn right side out. Press. Top stitch along the scalloped edge by machine (Fig. 4). Bring the ends together to form a circle and blindstitch the ends together.

6 Turn the bag (from step 4) right side out, and with right sides together, pin the scalloped fabric to the top of the bag. Machine sew them together (Fig. 5).

7 To make the handle, first, fuse the interfacing to the wrong side of the backing. Use spray adhesive to join 2 pieces of batting, fusible side out. Layer the backing and top with right sides together and place on top of the batting and pin together. Machine sew both sides of the handle. Trim the batting to 0.7 cm [¼"] and turn right side out. Machine quilt as shown (Fig. 6).

8 Pin the handles to the bag, matching the center points and the center of the handles, making sure the handles are not twisted. Sew them to the bag (Fig. 7).

9 Turn the scalloped edge up and fold the seam allowance and ends of the handle to the inside (Fig. 8).

10 Cut 6 pieces of fabric for the bag lining, and 6 pieces of lightweight interfacing (without any seam allowance). Fuse the interfacing to the wrong side of each lining piece. Sew the pieces (2 sets of A•B•C) together (step 3). Fold the seam allowance under, to the wrong side, at the top of the bag; press. Spray the wrong side of the lining with spray adhesive; insert the lining, wrong sides together, into the bag. Match the edges and seams at the top opening; blindstitch the lining to the inside of the outer bag (Fig. 9) to finish the bag.

◆ Fig. 1

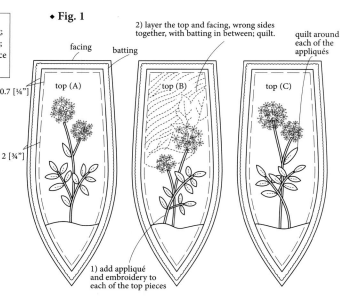

facing

batting

2) layer the top and facing, wrong sides together, with batting in between; quilt.

quilt around each of the appliqués

0.7 [¼"]

top (A)

top (B)

top (C)

2 [¾"]

1) add appliqué and embroidery to each of the top pieces

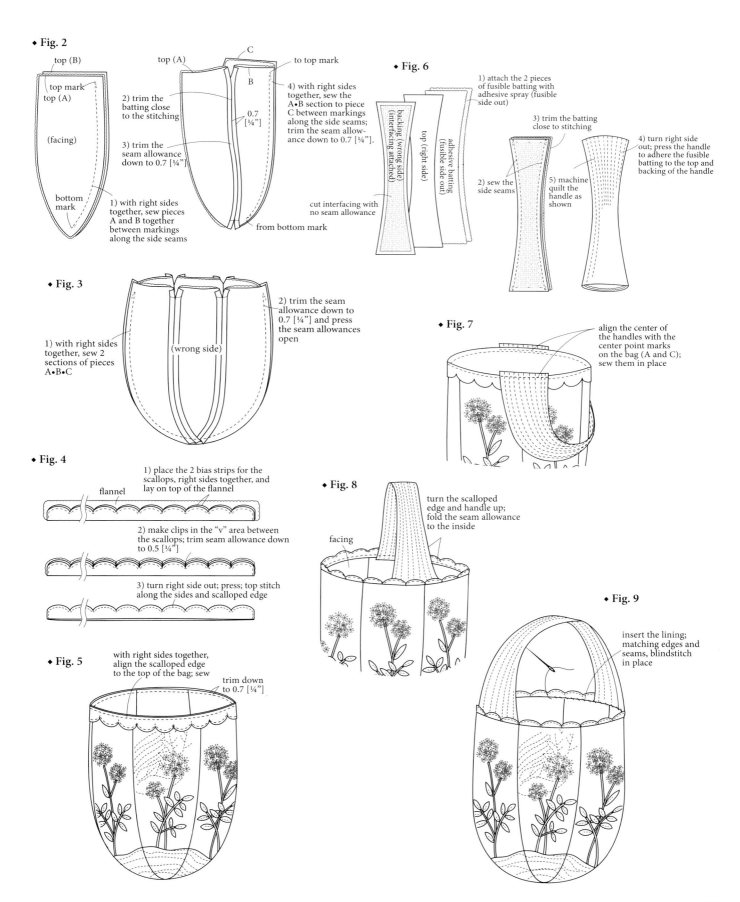

◆ Fig. 2

top (B)

top mark

top (A)

(facing)

bottom mark

1) with right sides together, sew pieces A and B together between markings along the side seams

C

top (A)

B

to top mark

2) trim the batting close to the stitching

3) trim the seam allowance down to 0.7 [¼"]

0.7 [¼"]

4) with right sides together, sew the A•B section to piece C between markings along the side seams; trim the seam allowance down to 0.7 [¼"].

from bottom mark

◆ Fig. 6

1) attach the 2 pieces of fusible batting with adhesive spray (fusible side out)

backing (wrong side) (interfacing attached)

top (right side)

adhesive batting (fusible side out)

cut interfacing with no seam allowance

2) sew the side seams

3) trim the batting close to stitching

5) machine quilt the handle as shown

4) turn right side out; press the handle to adhere the fusible batting to the top and backing of the handle

◆ Fig. 3

2) trim the seam allowance down to 0.7 [¼"] and press the seam allowances open

1) with right sides together, sew 2 sections of pieces A•B•C

(wrong side)

◆ Fig. 7

align the center of the handles with the center point marks on the bag (A and C); sew them in place

◆ Fig. 4

flannel

1) place the 2 bias strips for the scallops, right sides together, and lay on top of the flannel

2) make clips in the "v" area between the scallops; trim seam allowance down to 0.5 [¼"]

3) turn right side out; press; top stitch along the sides and scalloped edge

◆ Fig. 8

facing

turn the scalloped edge and handle up; fold the seam allowance to the inside

◆ Fig. 9

insert the lining; matching edges and seams, blindstitch in place

◆ Fig. 5

with right sides together, align the scalloped edge to the top of the bag; sew

trim down to 0.7 [¼"]

----- shown on p. 33

Marguerite Bag

❋ Finished Measurements:
  32 × 30 cm [12⅝" × 11¾"]
❋ The full-size template/pattern can be found on Side B of the pattern sheet inserts.

● Materials
Cottons
  Greenish-yellow print - 110 × 45 cm [43¼" × 17¾"] (top)
    - 2.5 × 118 cm [1" × 46½"] bias binding (handle openings)
  Green print - 110 × 80 cm [43¼" × 31½"] (backing)
  White/yellow - fat quarter or scraps (appliqué)
Batting - 110 × 50 cm [43¼" × 19¾"]
Embroidery thread - moss green

● Instructions
1 Cut out each of the bag pieces referring to the template/pattern and dimensional diagram. Trace the appliqué design directly onto the top front and top back of the bag using a marking pencil. Trace and cut out the appliqué patterns, adding

specified seam allowance*. Appliqué the designs to the top pieces and add the embroidery, referring to the pattern.
2 Layer the top and backing, wrong sides together, with the batting in between; baste. Quilt as shown, or as desired (Fig. 1). Remove the basting stitches, except for those around the edges. Repeat for the top back.
3 Mark and sew the darts on the backing of both the pieces. Press the darts toward the middle on the front piece, and toward the sides on the back piece; blindstitch them down to the backing (Fig. 2).
4 With right sides together, match the 2 handle areas for the front piece; pin in place and sew them together to create the handle (Fig. 3). Trim the top and batting seam allowances down to 0.7 cm [¼"]. Use the backing fabric to bind the raw edges; blindstitch down. Repeat for the back piece.
5 With right sides together, match the front and back pieces at the edges; pin in place. Sew the side seams around the outside on the finished sewing line (Fig. 4). Trim the seam allowances around the side, opening and handles down to 0.7 cm [¼"].
6 Make enough 2.5 cm [1"] wide bias binding to bind the side seam, the opening area and the two circular holes that make up the handles. Bind the side seam and blindstitch down to the backing.
7 Use the remainder of the bias binding to bind the opening and the two circular holes around the handles to finish the bag (Fig. 6).

● Dimensional Diagram

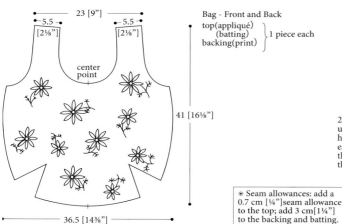

23 [9"]
5.5 [2⅛"]   5.5 [2⅛"]
center point
41 [16⅛"]
36.5 [14⅜"]

Bag - Front and Back
top(appliqué)
(batting)
backing(print) } 1 piece each

❋ Seam allowances: add a 0.7 cm [¼"]seam allowance to the top; add 3 cm[1¼"] to the backing and batting.

◆ Fig. 1

Bag Front (make the back in the same way)

batting
backing

2) quilt the background using a 1 cm [⅜"] cross-hatch pattern; quilt around each appliqué; remove all the basting, except around the edges

1) appliqué and embroider
0.7 [¼"]
3 [1¼"]

◆ Fig. 2

bag back (backing)

1) press and blindstitch the darts toward the sides on the back

batting

bag front (backing)

1) sew the darts

2) press and blindstitch the darts toward the middle on the front

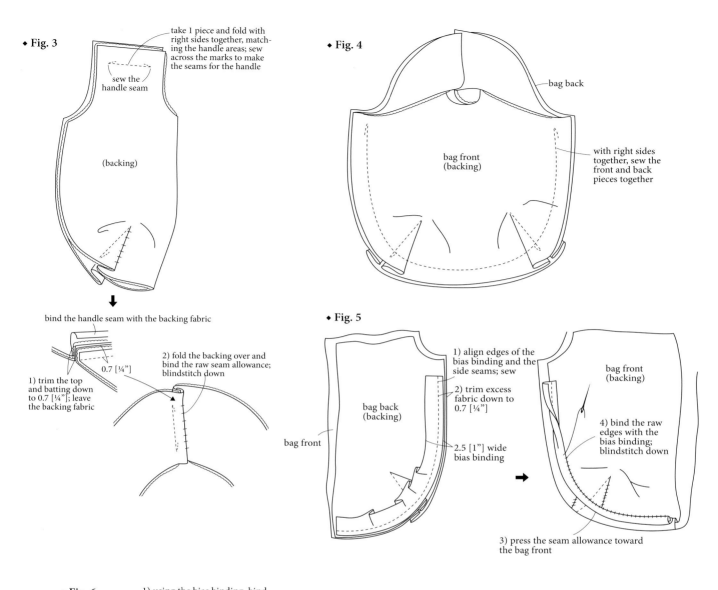

◆ Fig. 3

sew the handle seam

take 1 piece and fold with right sides together, matching the handle areas; sew across the marks to make the seams for the handle

(backing)

bind the handle seam with the backing fabric

1) trim the top and batting down to 0.7 [¼"]; leave the backing fabric

0.7 [¼"]

2) fold the backing over and bind the raw seam allowance; blindstitch down

◆ Fig. 4

bag back

bag front (backing)

with right sides together, sew the front and back pieces together

◆ Fig. 5

bag front

bag back (backing)

1) align edges of the bias binding and the side seams; sew

2) trim excess fabric down to 0.7 [¼"]

2.5 [1"] wide bias binding

bag front (backing)

4) bind the raw edges with the bias binding; blindstitch down

3) press the seam allowance toward the bag front

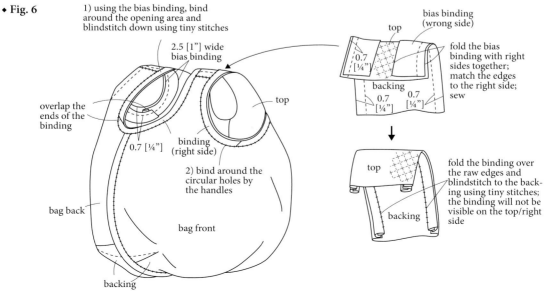

◆ Fig. 6

1) using the bias binding, bind around the opening area and blindstitch down using tiny stitches

2.5 [1"] wide bias binding

overlap the ends of the binding

0.7 [¼"]

binding (right side)

top

2) bind around the circular holes by the handles

bag back

bag front

backing

top

bias binding (wrong side)

0.7 [¼"]

backing

0.7 [¼"]   0.7 [¼"]

fold the bias binding with right sides together; match the edges to the right side; sew

top

backing

fold the binding over the raw edges and blindstitch to the backing using tiny stitches; the binding will not be visible on the top/right side

----- shown on p. 42

Barley Handbag

* Finished Measurements:
27 × 20 cm [10⅝" × 7⅞"]; 11 cm [4⅜"] gusset
* The full-size template/pattern can be found on
Side C of the pattern sheet inserts.

● Materials

Cottons
Beige print - 30 × 22 cm [11¾" × 8⅝"] (top front)
Grey print - 30 × 22 cm [11¾" × 8⅝"] (top back)
Grey print & homespun - 30 × 17 cm [11¾" × 6"] (gusset)
Brown homespun - 13 × 22 cm [5⅛" × 8⅝"] (bottom)
Beige homespun - 2 kinds - 30 × 7 cm each [11¾" × 2¾"] (handles)
Beige homespun - 110 × 35 cm each [43¼" × 13¾"] (backing, bottom
backing, bias binding for bottom)
Assorted fat quarters or scraps (appliqué)
Batting - 110 × 35 cm each [43¼" × 13¾"]
Fusible interfacing - 11 × 20 cm [4⅜" × 7⅞"]
Waxed cord - 60 cm [23⅝"]
Embroidery thread - dk green, dusky green

● Instructions

1 Cut out each of the bag pieces referring to the template/pattern and dimensional diagram. Piece together the bag front, and bag back with the gusset pieces. Trace the appliqué design directly onto the top front of the bag using a marking pencil. Trace and cut out the appliqué patterns, adding specified seam allowance*. Appliqué the designs to the top piece and add the embroidery, referring to the pattern (Fig. 1).
2 Make the handles for the bag, referring to Fig. 2.
3 Baste the handles in position on both the bag front and bag back. Referring to Fig. 3, place the bag top and backing with right sides together, sandwiching the handle in between; lay on top of the batting and sew across the top between markings. Turn the pieces right side out, so that the batting is between the top and the backing with the handle standing up. Baste; quilt as shown or as desired (Fig. 4).
4 Make the bottom of the bag, referring to Fig. 5.
5 Refer to p. 47 and 48 (Cow Parsnip Handbag) for directions on how to sew the bag bottom to the front and back and finish the seam allowances (Fig. 6).
6 Turn the bag right side out. Referring to Fig. 7, press the side seams together and top stitch 0.2 cm [¹⁄₁₆"] along each of the 4 seams from top to bottom by machine.

● Dimensional Diagram

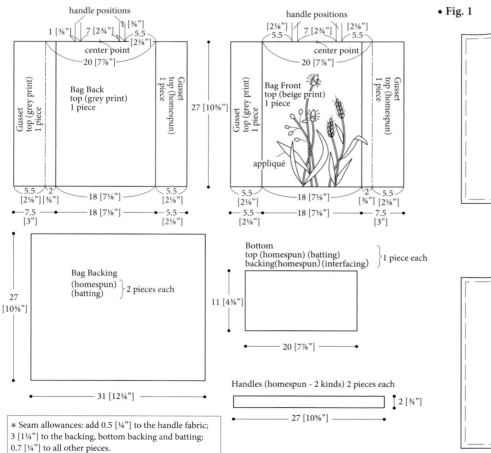

* Seam allowances: add 0.5 [¼"] to the handle fabric;
3 [1¼"] to the backing, bottom backing and batting;
0.7 [¼"] to all other pieces.

◆ Fig. 1

2) appliqué and embroider the design

bag front

1) sew the gussets to the bag front and the bag back

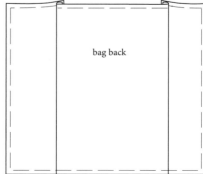

bag back

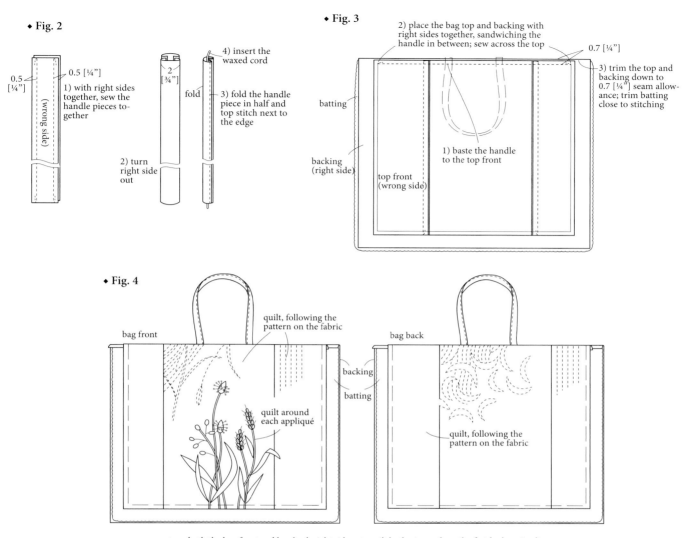

◆ Fig. 2

0.5 [¼"]
0.5 [¼"]

(wrong side)

1) with right sides together, sew the handle pieces together

2) turn right side out

2 [¾"]

fold

4) insert the waxed cord

3) fold the handle piece in half and top stitch next to the edge

◆ Fig. 3

2) place the bag top and backing with right sides together, sandwiching the handle in between; sew across the top

0.7 [¼"]

3) trim the top and backing down to 0.7 [¼"] seam allowance; trim batting close to stitching

batting

backing (right side)

top front (wrong side)

1) baste the handle to the top front

◆ Fig. 4

bag front

quilt, following the pattern on the fabric

bag back

backing

batting

quilt around each appliqué

quilt, following the pattern on the fabric

turn both the bag front and bag back right side out; quilt both pieces; draw the finished sewing line on the backing of both pieces

◆ Fig. 5

batting

backing (wrong side)

bottom (right side)

1) iron on the fusible interfacing

2) machine quilt

3) draw the finished sewing line on the backing

◆ Fig. 6

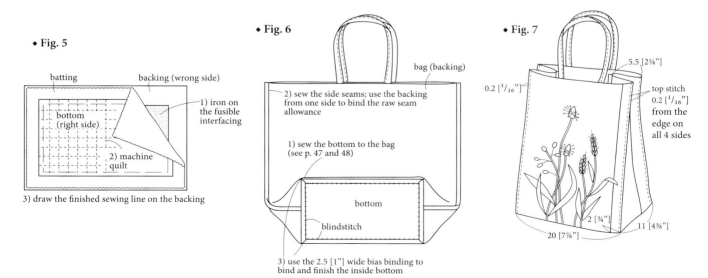

bag (backing)

2) sew the side seams; use the backing from one side to bind the raw seam allowance

1) sew the bottom to the bag (see p. 47 and 48)

bottom

blindstitch

3) use the 2.5 [1"] wide bias binding to bind and finish the inside bottom

◆ Fig. 7

5.5 [2⅛"]

0.2 [1/16"]

top stitch 0.2 [1/16"] from the edge on all 4 sides

2 [¾"]

20 [7⅞"]

11 [4⅜"]

----- shown on p. 43

Peeping Down from Above

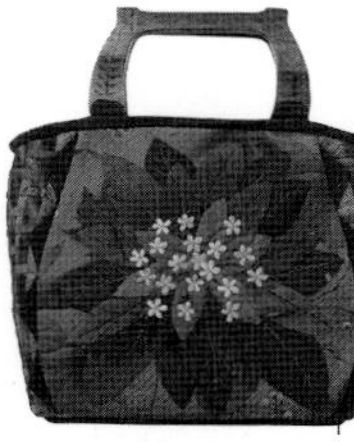

∗ Finished Measurements:
27 × 23 cm [10⅝ × 9"]; 9.5 × 22.5 cm [3¾" × 8⅞"] bag bottom

∗ The full-size template/pattern can be found on Side D of the pattern sheet inserts.

• Materials

Cottons

- Beige print - 26 × 55 cm [10¼" × 21⅝"] (top front and back)
- Beige homespun - 30 × 38 cm [11¾" × 15"] (gusset, top zipper opening)
- Brown homespun - 110 × 50 cm each [43¼" × 19¾"] (bottom, triangle accents, handle loops, bias binding around opening)
- Beige print - 2 kinds - 110 × 50 cm each [43¼" × 19¾"] (backing)
- Muslin - 16 × 30 cm each [6¼" × 11¾"] (for the bottom facing)
- 2 contrasting prints - 1.2 cm × 250 cm [½" × 98½"] bias tape (gusset weave)
  0.6 cm × 420 cm [¼" × 165⅜"] bias tape (gusset weave)
- Assorted fat quarters or scraps (appliqué)

Batting - 110 × 50 cm each [43¼" × 19¾"]
Fusible interfacing - 13 × 55 cm [4⅜" × 21⅝"]
Flannel - 25 × 15 cm [9¾" × 6¾"]
Waxed cord (grey) - 20 cm [7⅞"]
Embroidery thread - 3 shades of green (dk~lt), yellow
Handle - 1 pair
1 Zipper - 26 cm [10¼"] long
Spray adhesive

• Instructions

1 Cut out each of the bag pieces referring to the template/pattern and dimensional diagram. Trace the appliqué design directly onto the top front of the bag using a marking pencil. Trace and cut out the appliqué patterns, adding specified seam allowance*. Appliqué the designs to the top and add the embroidery, referring to the pattern. Layer the top and backing, wrong sides together, with the batting in between; baste. Quilt as shown, or as desired (Fig. 1).

2 Using the bias tape makers, make the 1.2 cm [½"] and 0.6 cm [¼"] wide bias tape to make the basket weave for the gussets (Basics 4, p. 21).

3 Refer to Fig. 2 to make the gussets. With the gusset piece as a base, weave the lengths of 2 different bias tapes, as shown, to create the basket weave. Blindstitch each of the lengths of bias tape to the base gusset fabric. Layer the woven gusset top and backing, wrong sides together, with the batting in between; baste. Quilt as shown, or as desired.

4 Referring to Fig. 3, make the 4 pieces that will become the triangle accents.

5 With right sides together and edges matching, sandwich the triangle accents between the bag and gusset pieces and sew the side seams to create a cylinder shape (Fig. 4).

6 Make the 2 bottom sections of the bag (A, B) by referring to Fig. 5.

7 To make the top zipper opening piece (Fig. 6), refer to the Fennel Mini Pouch directions on p. 92, 93.

8 With right sides together and matching the edges, seams and marks, sew the quilted bottom piece (A) to the bottom of the bag. Trim the seam allowance down to 0.7 [¼"]. Press the seam allowance on the backing piece (B) toward the interfacing, making sure that when placed against the bag bottom (A), it will cover the facing. Spray the wrong side with spray adhesive and attach it to the bottom facing. Blindstitch it in place (Fig. 7).

9 Make the 4 handle loops and insert them through the handles in the same way as for the Olive Bag on p. 86, 87 (Fig. 8).

10 With wrong sides together and matching edges and marks, pin the zipper opening piece to the top opening of the bag, sandwiching the handle loops in position (Fig. 9). Sew all the way around. Trim the seam allowance down to 0.7 [¼"] and bind the raw edges with the bias binding (Fig. 10) to complete the bag.

• Dimensional Diagram

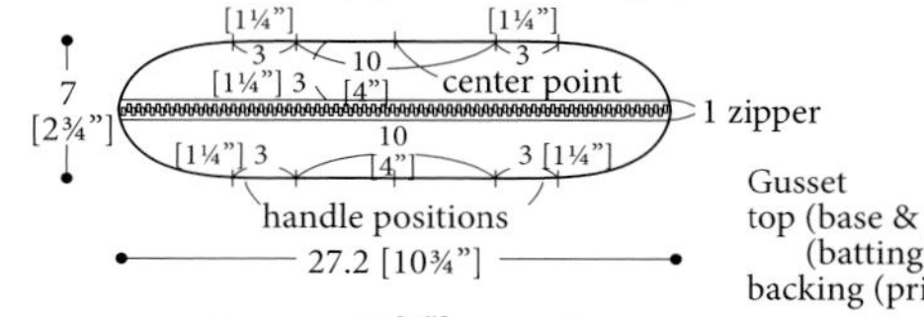
Top Zipper Opening
top (homespun) (batting)
backing (print) (interfacing)
2 pieces each
center point
1 zipper
handle positions
27.2 [10¾"]
7 [2¾"]

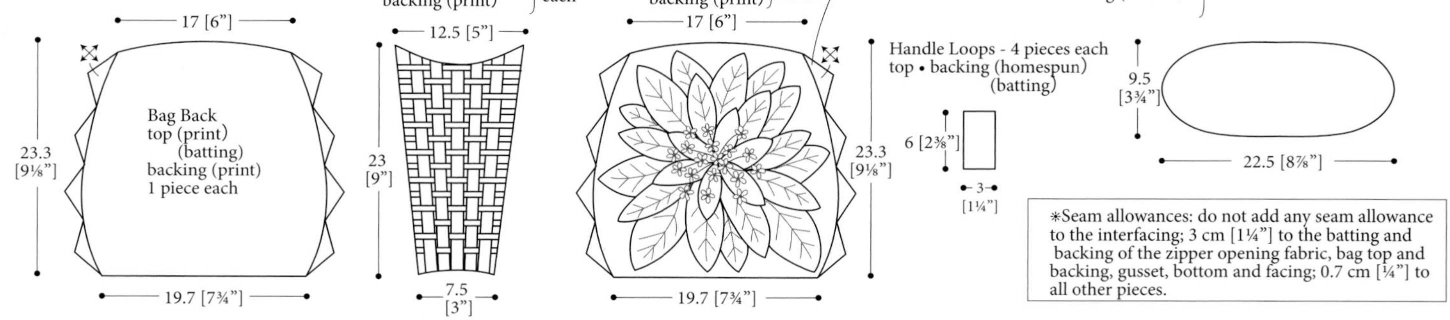
Bag Back
top (print)
(batting)
backing (print)
1 piece each
17 [6"]
23.3 [9⅛"]
19.7 [7¾"]
Gusset
top (base & weave)
(batting)
backing (print)
2 pieces each
12.5 [5"]
23 [9"]
7.5 [3"]
Bag Front
top (appliqué)
(batting)
backing (print)
1 piece each
17 [6"]
23.3 [9⅛"]
19.7 [7¾"]
Triangle Accents
top • backing
(homespun)
(flannel)
4 pieces each
Handle Loops - 4 pieces each
top • backing (homespun)
(batting)
6 [2⅜"]
3 [1¼"]
Bottom
top (homespun)
(interfacing)
(batting)
facing (muslin)
1 piece each
Bottom Lining
backing (print)
(interfacing)
1 piece each
9.5 [3¾"]
22.5 [8⅞"]

∗Seam allowances: do not add any seam allowance to the interfacing; 3 cm [1¼"] to the batting and backing of the zipper opening fabric, bag top and backing, gusset, bottom and facing; 0.7 cm [¼"] to all other pieces.

◆ Fig. 1

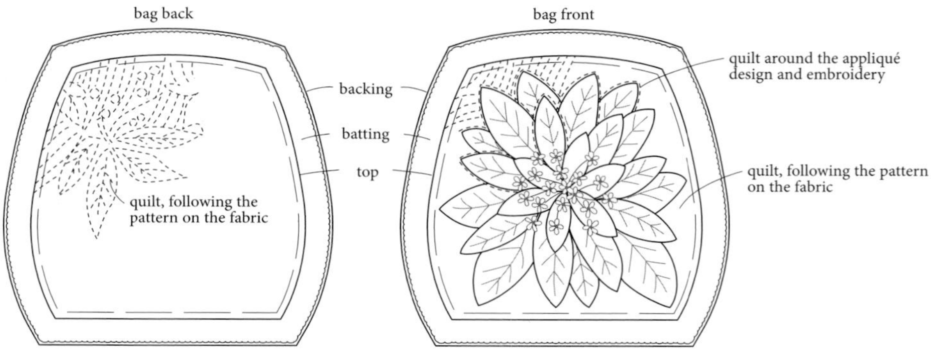
bag back
bag front
backing
batting
top
quilt, following the pattern on the fabric
quilt around the appliqué design and embroidery
quilt, following the pattern on the fabric

◆ **Fig. 2**

1) align the 1.2 [½"] bias tape first; pin in place

2) weave the 0.6 [¼"] bias tape as shown

3) blindstitch each length of bias tape to the top base

4) make a quilt sandwich

backing

batting

quilt within each area made by the bias tape

5) trace the finished sewing line of the gusset on the backing

◆ **Fig. 3**

flannel

2) make snips into the "v" of the zigzag

3) trim the flannel close to the stitching

(wrong side)

1) lay the top and backing with right sides together; lay the wrong side of the backing on top of the flannel; sew

4) turn right side out; top stitch by machine

◆ **Fig. 4**

gusset

finished sewing line

bag (backing)

blindstitch up to 1 cm [⅜"] past the finished sewing line

1) with right sides together and sandwiching the triangle accents piece between, pin the bag and gussets together; sew from top to bottom

2) trim the top and batting down to 0.7 [¼"]; use the gusset backing to bind the raw edges

◆ **Fig. 5**

top (right side)

batting

facing (wrong side)

bottom (A)

1) iron the interfacing to the wrong side of the facing

2) with wrong sides together, layer the top and bottom with batting between; quilt

backing (wrong side)

3) iron on interfacing

bottom (B) (backing)

◆ **Fig. 6**

zipper

backing   batting   top   machine quilt

◆ **Fig. 8**

top stitch

make 4 handle loops

◆ **Fig. 9**

3) insert the handle loops in position; sew around the edge; press the seam allowance toward the outside

1) with wrong sides together, sew the zipper opening and bag pieces together

2) with right sides together, align the 3.5 [1⅜"] bias binding on the edge and pin in place

bag (top)

zipper opening piece

◆ **Fig. 7**

4) blindstitch around the edges to secure the inside bottom backing

1) sew the quilted bottom piece (A) to the bag with right sides together; trim the seam allowance down to 0.7 [¼"] and press toward the bottom

2) press the seam allowance on the bottom backing (B) under toward the interfacing

3) spray the wrong side with spray adhesive

◆ **Fig. 10**

blindstitch   blindstitch

3) thread the waxed cord through the zipper; attach bead and tie off to make the zipper pull

2) bring handles up; blindstitch the handle loops edges to the binding

1) trim down to 0.7 [¼"] seam allowance; bind the raw edges around the opening with the bias binding and blindstitch

----- shown on p. 50

Oak Leaves &Acorn Bag

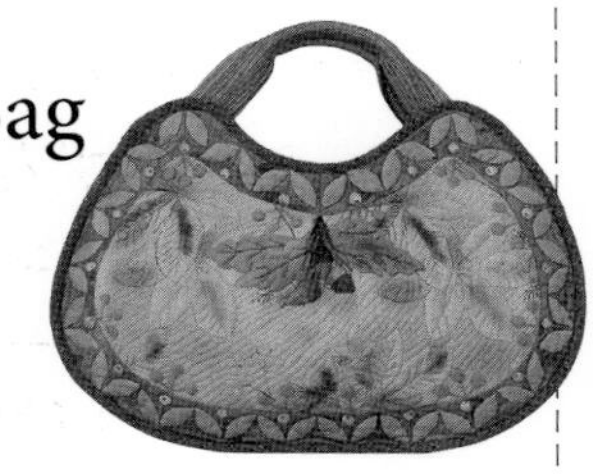

✻ Finished Measurements:
26 × 39 cm [10¼ × 15⅜"]; 5 cm [2"] gusset
✻ The full-size template/pattern can be found
on Side B of the pattern sheet inserts.

Materials

Cottons
    Beige print - 23 × 75 cm [9" × 29½"] (top A)
    Grey print - 36 × 90 cm [14⅛" × 35⅜"] (top B, gusset)
    Beige homespun - 90 × 45 cm [35⅜" × 17¾"] (backing)
    Grey homespun - 35 × 35 cm each [13¾" × 13¾"] (handles)
    Grey homespun - 3.5 cm × 220 cm [1⅜" × 86⅝"] bias binding
    Assorted fat quarters or scraps (appliqué)
Batting - 90 × 45 cm [35⅜" × 17¾"]
Fusible interfacing - 5 × 75 cm [2" × 29½"]
Woven nylon webbing - 3 × 58 cm [1¼" × 22⅞"]
Embroidery thread - 2 shades of green (dk, lt)

● Instructions

1 Cut out each of the bag pieces referring to the template/pattern and dimensional diagram. Fold the seam allowance of top B under 0.7 cm [¼"] and center on top of top A; pin in place and blindstitch down to create the bag front. Repeat for the bag back.

2 Trace the appliqué design directly onto the top front of the bag using a marking pencil. Trace and cut out the appliqué patterns, adding specified seam allowance*. Appliqué the designs to the top and add the embroidery, referring to the pattern.

3 Layer the top and backing, wrong sides together, with the batting in between; baste. Quilt as shown, or as desired (Fig. 1).

4 After the pieces are quilted, they will have likely shrunk somewhat. Resize the bag outline paper pattern down to fit within the quilted pieces, allowing for a 0.7 [¼"] seam allowance all around. Draw the new finished sewing line on the top of the bag pieces.

5 Make the gusset (Fig. 2). When completed, draw the finished sewing line on the right side of the top.

6 Referring to Fig. 3, make a pleat in the center of both the bag front and back.

7 With wrong sides together, sew the bag front to the gusset along the finished sewing lines, matching edges and markings; repeat for the bag back.

8 Make the bias binding and use it to bind the raw edges of both seams (Fig. 4).

9 Sew the 2 handles referring to Fig. 5.

10 Position the handles in place on the inside top opening of both sides. Sew them in place, catching the batting as you blindstitch (Fig. 6) to complete the bag.

● Dimensional Diagram

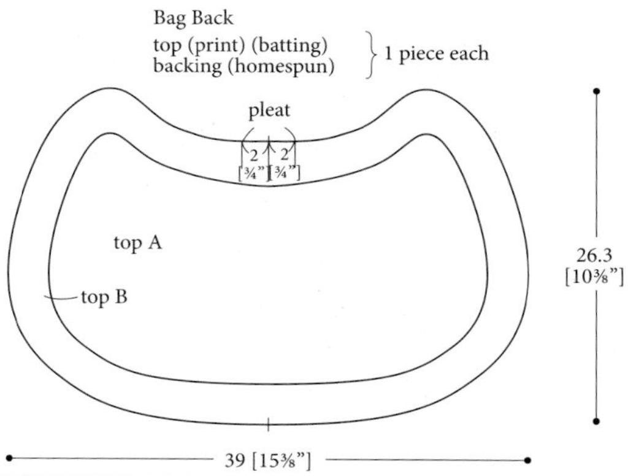

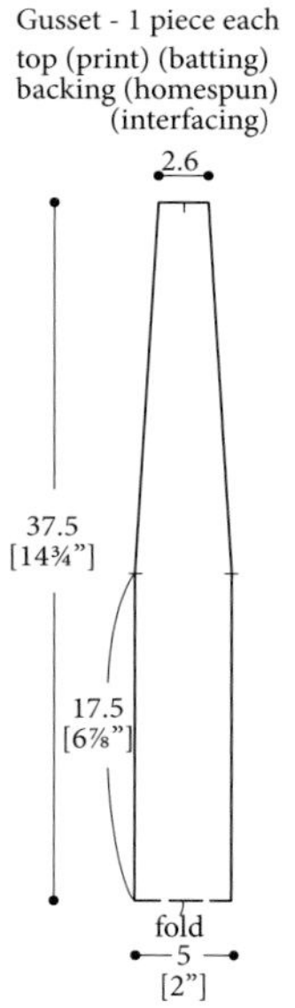

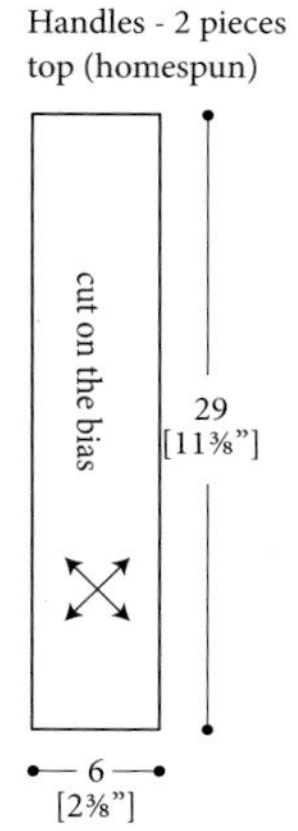

Bag Back
top (print) (batting)
backing (homespun) } 1 piece each

pleat
2 [¾"] 2 [¾"]

top A
top B

26.3 [10⅜"]

39 [15⅜"]

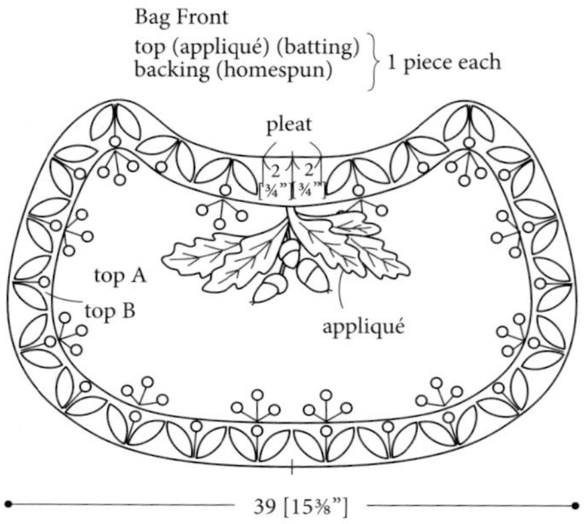

✻ Seam allowances: add 3 cm [1¼"] to the backing and batting;
0.7 cm [¼"] to all other pieces; do not add any seam allowance
to the interfacing.

Bag Front
top (appliqué) (batting)
backing (homespun) } 1 piece each

pleat
2 [¾"] 2 [¾"]

top A
top B
appliqué

39 [15⅜"]

Gusset - 1 piece each
top (print) (batting)
backing (homespun)
(interfacing)

2.6

37.5 [14¾"]

17.5 [6⅞"]

fold
5 [2"]

Handles - 2 pieces
top (homespun)

cut on the bias

29 [11⅜"]

6 [2⅜"]

◆ Fig. 1

bag back
backing
batting
0.7 [¼"]

quilting
quilt, following the pattern on the fabric
quilt diagonal lines, freehand

3) draw the finished sewing line on the top side of both pieces

bag front

1) do the appliqué and the embroidery

2) with wrong sides together, layer the top and backing with batting in between; baste and quilt

quilt along the edge

quilt around each appliqué

quilt, following the pattern on the fabric

quilt diagonal lines, freehand

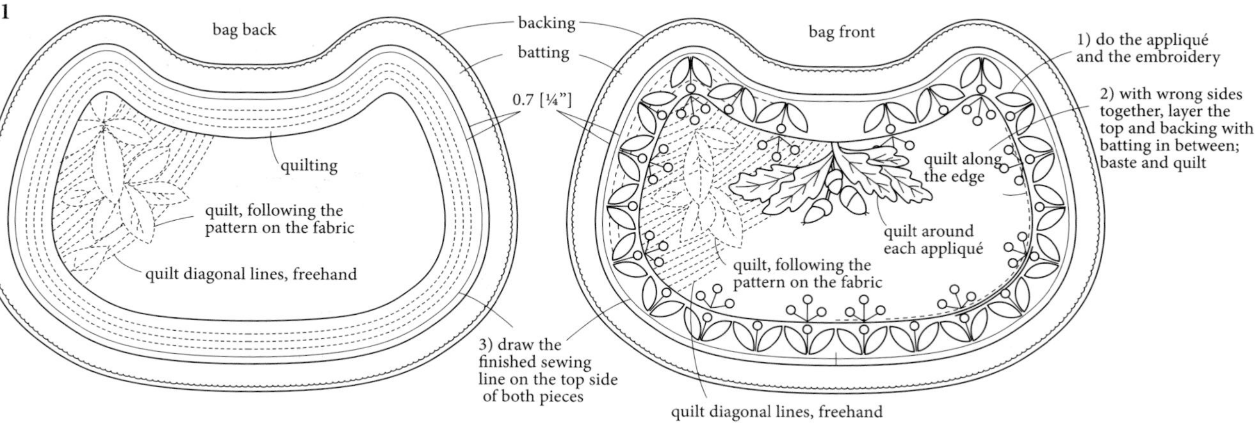

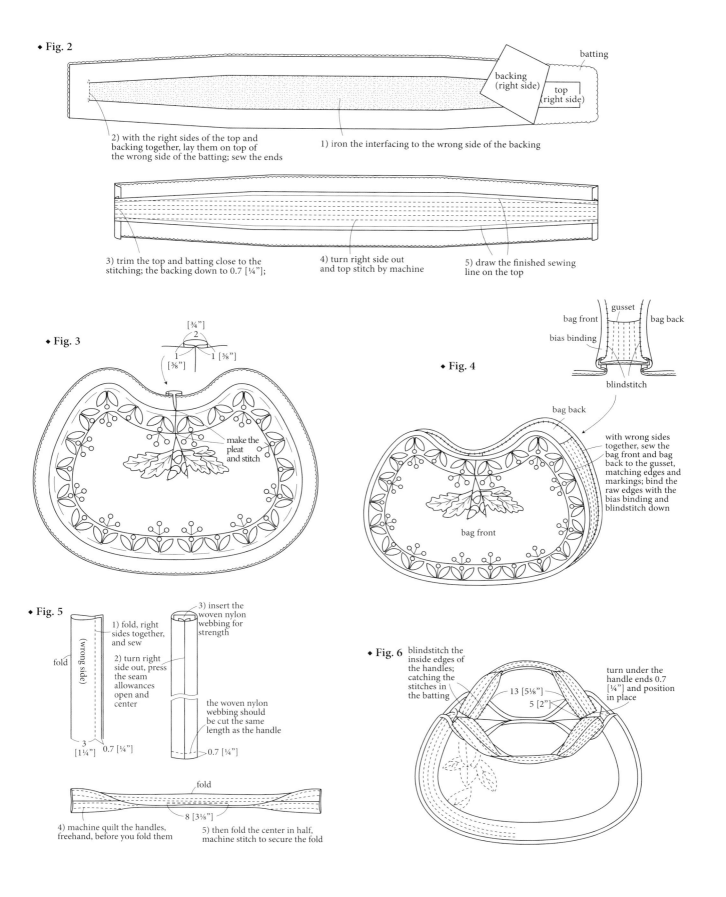

◆ Fig. 2

batting

backing (right side)

top (right side)

2) with the right sides of the top and backing together, lay them on top of the wrong side of the batting; sew the ends

1) iron the interfacing to the wrong side of the backing

3) trim the top and batting close to the stitching; the backing down to 0.7 [¼"];

4) turn right side out and top stitch by machine

5) draw the finished sewing line on the top

◆ Fig. 3

[¾"]
2
1   1 [⅜"]
[⅜"]

make the pleat and stitch

◆ Fig. 4

gusset
bag front   bag back
bias binding

blindstitch

bag back

with wrong sides together, sew the bag front and bag back to the gusset, matching edges and markings; bind the raw edges with the bias binding and blindstitch down

bag front

◆ Fig. 5

fold

(wrong side)

1) fold, right sides together, and sew

2) turn right side out, press the seam allowances open and center

3) insert the woven nylon webbing for strength

the woven nylon webbing should be cut the same length as the handle

0.7 [¼"]

3 [1¼"]   0.7 [¼"]

fold

8 [3⅛"]

4) machine quilt the handles, freehand, before you fold them

5) then fold the center in half, machine stitch to secure the fold

◆ Fig. 6

blindstitch the inside edges of the handles; catching the stitches in the batting

13 [5⅛"]
5 [2"]

turn under the handle ends 0.7 [¼"] and position in place

----- shown on p. 51

Horse Chestnut Tote

✳ Finished Measurements:
26 × 30 cm [10¼" × 11¾"]; 13 × 32 cm [5⅛" × 12⅝"] bag bottom
✳ The full-size template/pattern can be found on
Side B of the pattern sheet inserts.

● Materials

Cottons
Dk brown print - 90 × 50 cm [35⅜" × 19¾"] (top)
Grey homespun - 110 × 55 cm [43¼" × 21⅝"] (backing)
Dk brown homespun - 35 × 35 cm each [13¾" × 13¾"] (bottom)
Muslin - 40 × 20 cm each [15¾" × 7⅞"] (facing for the bottom)
Print - 3.5 cm × 200 cm [1⅜" × 78¾"] bias binding (for handle openings)
Assorted fat quarters or scraps (appliqué for leaves, nuts, branches)
Batting - 110 × 55 cm [43¼" × 21⅝"]
Embroidery thread - moss green, yellow-ochre, brown, dk brown

● Instructions

1 Cut out each of the bag pieces referring to the template/pattern and dimensional diagram. Trace the appliqué design directly onto the top front of the bag
using a marking pencil.

2 Trace and cut out the appliqué patterns, adding specified seam allowance*.
Appliqué the designs to the top and add the embroidery, referring to the pattern
(Fig. 1).

● Dimensional Diagram

3 Layer the top and backing, wrong sides together, with the batting in between;
baste. Quilt as shown, or as desired. Make the bag back without adding the
appliqué or embroidery (Fig. 1, 2).

4 With right sides together, match the 2 handle areas for the front piece; pin in
place and sew them together to create the handle (Fig. 3, p. 74, 75). Trim the top
and batting seam allowances down to 0.7 cm [¼"]. Use the backing fabric to
bind the raw edges; blindstitch down. Repeat for the handle area on the back
piece.

5 With right sides together, sew the bag front and bag back together along the
side seams. Trim the top and batting; bind the seams using the backing fabric
by folding it over the raw seam allowances and blindstitching down toward the
front (Fig. 4).

6 To make the bottom of the bag, layer the top and facing (fused with interfacing), wrong sides together, with the batting in between; baste. Quilt as shown,
or as desired (Fig. 5).

7 With right sides together, sew the bottom to the bag, easing in the fullness as
you sew. Trim the seam allowance down to 0.7 cm [¼"] and press toward the
bottom (Fig. 6).

8 After the bottom piece is quilted (from Fig. 5), it will have likely shrunk
somewhat. Resize the bottom outline paper pattern down to fit over the seam,
allowing for a 0.7 [¼"] seam allowance all around. Cut out the bottom backing
piece and fuse the interfacing to the wrong side. Press the seam allowance on
the backing piece toward the interfacing, making sure that when placed against
the bag bottom, it will cover the facing. Spray the wrong side with spray adhesive and attach it to the bottom facing. Blindstitch it in place to cover the stitches (Fig. 7).

9 Make the bias binding and bind the raw seam allowances around the handle
opening areas (Fig. 8, p. 74, 75). Fold the center of the handles in half; whipstitch together to complete the bag (Fig. 8).

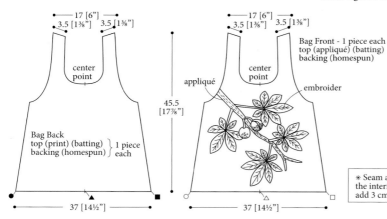

Bottom (top) - 1 piece each
top (homespun) (batting)
facing (muslin) (interfacing)

Bottom (backing) - 1 piece each
backing (homespun)
(interfacing)

bottom
cut on the bias

13 [5⅛"]

32 [12⅝"]

Bag Front - 1 piece each
top (appliqué) (batting)
backing (homespun)

appliqué

center
point

embroider

Bag Back
top (print) (batting)
backing (homespun) } 1 piece each

center
point

45.5 [17⅞"]

17 [6"]
3.5 [1⅜"]   3.5 [1⅜"]

37 [14½"]

17 [6"]
3.5 [1⅜"]   3.5 [1⅜"]

37 [14½"]

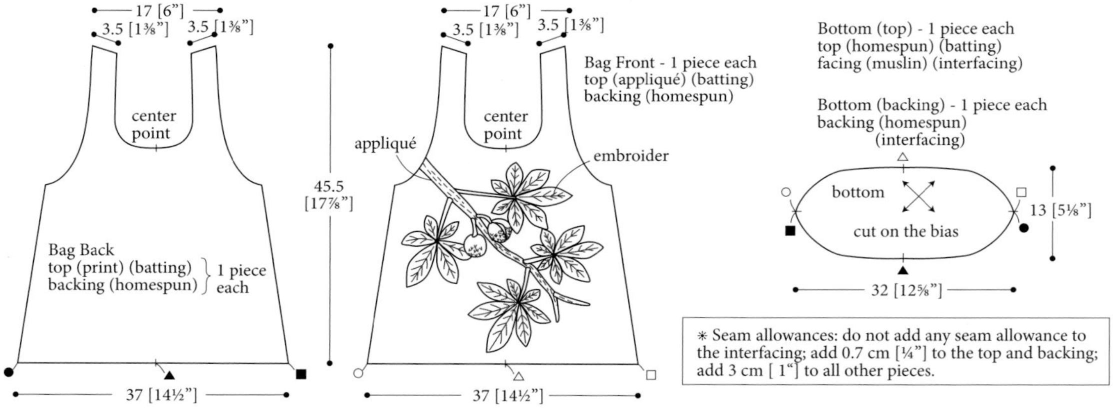

✳ Seam allowances: do not add any seam allowance to
the interfacing; add 0.7 cm [¼"] to the top and backing;
add 3 cm [1"] to all other pieces.

◆ Fig. 1

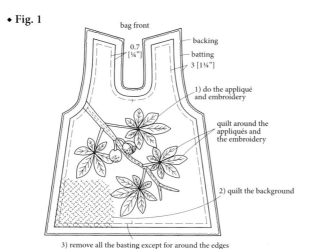

bag front

0.7 [¼"]

backing
batting
3 [1¼"]

1) do the appliqué
and embroidery

quilt around the
appliqués and
the embroidery

2) quilt the background

3) remove all the basting except for around the edges

◆ Fig. 2

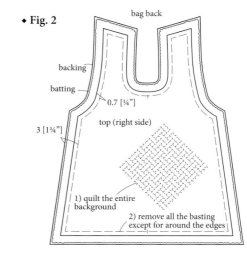

bag back

backing

batting

0.7 [¼"]

3 [1¼"]

top (right side)

1) quilt the entire
background

2) remove all the basting
except for around the edges

82

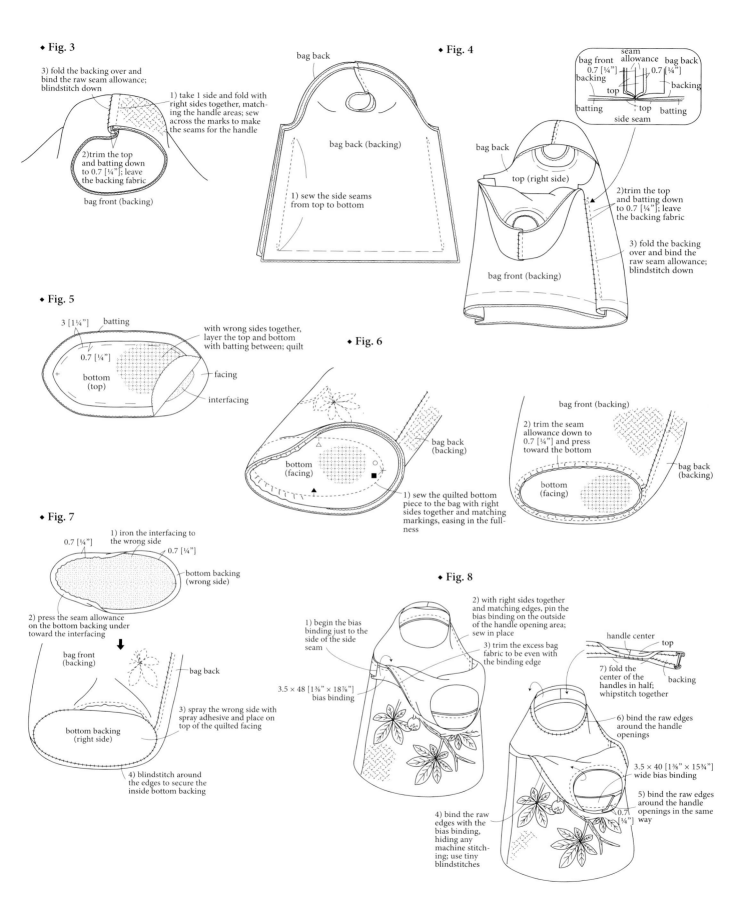

◆ Fig. 3

3) fold the backing over and bind the raw seam allowance; blindstitch down

1) take 1 side and fold with right sides together, matching the handle areas; sew across the marks to make the seams for the handle

2) trim the top and batting down to 0.7 [¼"]; leave the backing fabric

bag front (backing)

◆ Fig. 4

bag back

bag back (backing)

1) sew the side seams from top to bottom

seam allowance
bag front   bag back
0.7 [¼"]   0.7 [¼"]
backing   backing
top   top
batting   top   batting
side seam

bag back

top (right side)

2) trim the top and batting down to 0.7 [¼"]; leave the backing fabric

3) fold the backing over and bind the raw seam allowance; blindstitch down

bag front (backing)

◆ Fig. 5

3 [1¼"]   batting

0.7 [¼"]

bottom (top)

with wrong sides together, layer the top and bottom with batting between; quilt

facing

interfacing

◆ Fig. 6

bottom (facing)

bag back (backing)

1) sew the quilted bottom piece to the bag with right sides together and matching markings, easing in the fullness

bag front (backing)

2) trim the seam allowance down to 0.7 [¼"] and press toward the bottom

bottom (facing)

bag back (backing)

◆ Fig. 7

0.7 [¼"]   1) iron the interfacing to the wrong side
0.7 [¼"]

bottom backing (wrong side)

2) press the seam allowance on the bottom backing under toward the interfacing

bag front (backing)

bag back

3) spray the wrong side with spray adhesive and place on top of the quilted facing

bottom backing (right side)

4) blindstitch around the edges to secure the inside bottom backing

◆ Fig. 8

1) begin the bias binding just to the side of the side seam

3.5 × 48 [1⅜" × 18⅞"] bias binding

2) with right sides together and matching edges, pin the bias binding on the outside of the handle opening area; sew in place

3) trim the excess bag fabric to be even with the binding edge

4) bind the raw edges with the bias binding, hiding any machine stitching; use tiny blindstitches

handle center   top

backing

7) fold the center of the handles in half; whipstitch together

6) bind the raw edges around the handle openings

3.5 × 40 [1⅜" × 15¾"] wide bias binding

5) bind the raw edges around the handle openings in the same way

0.7 [¼"]

----- shown on p. 52

Mountain Ash Bag

❉ Finished Measurements:
36 × 34 cm [14⅛" × 13⅜"]
❉ The full-size template/pattern can be found on
Side B of the pattern sheet inserts.

● Materials
Cottons
   Dk green print - 90 × 40 cm [35⅜" × 15¾"] (bag top, handle top)
   Beige homespun - 110 × 80 cm [43¼" × 31½"] (backing, tabs, bias binding
   for inner seams and handle opening)
   Assorted fat quarters or scraps (appliqué)
Batting - 100 × 45 cm [39⅜" × 17¾"]
Fusible interfacing - 10 × 40 cm [4" × 15¾"]
Embroidery thread - brown, black
Magnetic closure - 1.5 cm [⅝"] 1 set

● Instructions

1 Cut out each of the bag pieces referring to the template/pattern and dimensional diagram. Trace the appliqué design directly onto the top front of the bag using a marking pencil.

2 Trace and cut out the appliqué patterns, adding specified seam allowance*. Cut the stems out of 1 cm [⅜"] wide bias strips and appliqué, referring to Basics 6 (p. 21). Appliqué the leaves and berries to the top and add the embroidery, referring to the pattern. Layer the top and backing, wrong sides together, with the batting in between; baste. Quilt as shown, or as desired. Make the bag back without adding the appliqué or embroidery (Fig. 1, 2).

3 Draw the finished sewing line of the bag outline on the backing of the bag front and bag back and sew the darts that are marked. With right sides together, pin the bag front and back in place and sew the side seams together. Trim the seam allowances down to 0.7 cm [¼"]. Make a 2.5 × 48 cm [1" × 18⅞"] wide bias binding and bind the side seams; blindstitch down (Fig. 3).

4 Make the handle, cut out the pieces; appliqué and embroider the top piece, then make a quilt sandwich and quilt as shown, or as desired (Fig. 4).

5 With right sides together, sew the handle to the bag, making sure that the stem appliqués from both pieces line up perfectly. Use 2 pieces of 13 cm [5⅛"] of the 2.5 cm [1"] wide bias binding to finish the handle seams (Fig. 5).

6 Make the tabs for the magnetic closures by referring to Fig. 6.

7 Use a 2.5 × 70 cm [1" × 27½"] bias binding to bind the bag opening. With right side together, lay it against the right side of the opening; pin in place, matching edges and sew along the finished sewing line. Sew the tabs in place on the backing (Fig. 7).

8 Trim the seam allowances down to 0.7 [¼"]; fold the binding over to the backing side; blindstitch in place to complete the bag (Fig. 7).

● Dimensional Diagram

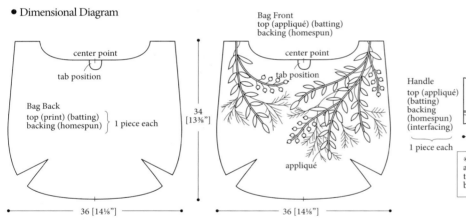

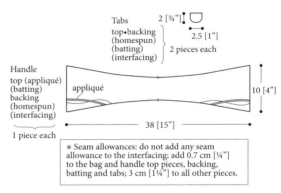

✻ Seam allowances: do not add any seam allowance to the interfacing; add 0.7 cm [¼"] to the bag and handle top pieces, backing, batting and tabs; 3 cm [1¼"] to all other pieces.

◆ Fig. 1

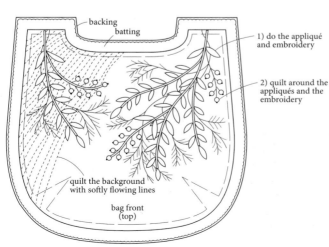

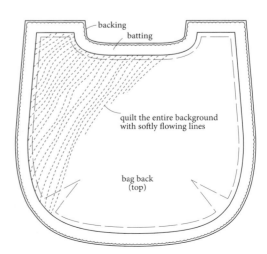

84

◆ Fig. 2

sew just
beyond
the finished
sewing line

1 [⅜"]

1) draw the finished sewing line
on the backing of both pieces

bag front

5) place the bag front and back
with right sides together and
sew the side seams

2) sew the darts

3) press the darts on
bag front toward the
middle and blindstitch
down

4) press the darts on the bag back toward the
side seams and blindstitch down

◆ Fig. 3

bind the seams with the bias
binding; press it toward the
back and blindstitch down

bag back

◆ Fig. 4

1) appliqué and embroider
the top fabric of the handle

3) machine quilt, freehand

4) draw the
finished sewing
line on the
backing

(wrong side)

2) iron the interfacing to
the wrong side of the backing

batting

backing

top

◆ Fig. 5

handle

2) bind the seam
with bias binding;
press toward the
handle and blind-
stitch down

1) with right sides
together, sew the
handle to the bag

bag back

bag front

side seam

◆ Fig. 6

batting

top (right side)

1) iron inter-
facing to the
wrong side of
the backing

2) sew
around the
sides and
bottom

3) trim the
batting close
to stitching

4) ease the
seam allowance
around the curve

magnetic
closure

5) turn right side
out and insert the
magnetic closure;
1 in each tab

◆ Fig. 7

bind the opening with
the 2.5 [1"] wide bias
binding; turn right
side out

on the right side,
connect the
embroidery design
between the handle
and the bag

blindstitch

sew the tabs down and
around the magnetic closure

backing

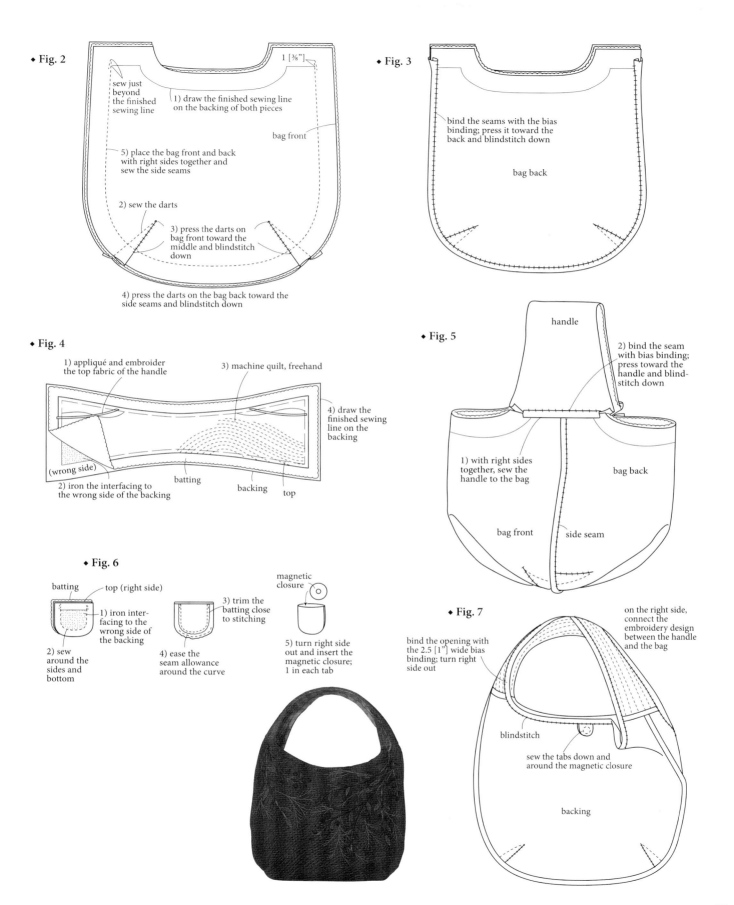

----- shown on p. 53

Olive Handbag

✳ Finished Measurements:
31 × 38.5 cm [12¼" × 15⅛"]
✳ The full-size template/pattern can be found on
Side B of the pattern sheet inserts.

● Materials

Cottons
　Beige print - 110 × 26 cm [43¼" × 10¼"]　(lower bag top)
　Lt green print - 110 × 27 cm [43¼" × 10⅝"]　(upper bag top and facing)
　Beige print - 110 × 60 cm [43¼" × 23⅝"]　(lower bag backing, bias binding)
　Brown print - 9 × 17 cm [3½" × 6"]　(handle loops)
　Muslin - 90 × 18 cm [35⅜" × 7⅛"]　(facing for upper bag top)
　Assorted fat quarters or scraps (appliqué)
Batting - 110 × 50 cm [43¼" × 19¾"]
Heavyweight fusible interfacing - 45 × 80 cm [17¾" × 31½"]
Lightweight fusible interfacing - 23 × 80 cm [9" × 31½"]
Embroidery thread - green
Handles - 1 pair
Magnetic closure - 1.5 cm [⅝"] 1 set

● Dimensional Diagram

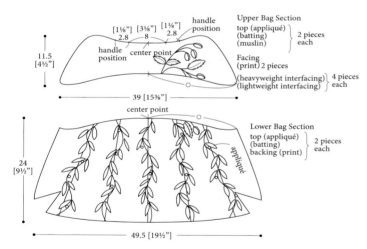

✳ Seam allowances: do not add any seam allowance
to the interfacing; add 0.7 cm [¼"] to the top, facings,
handle loops, backing and batting; add 3 cm [1¼"] to
all other pieces.

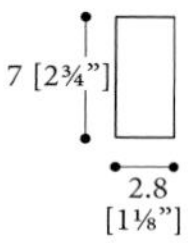

Handle Loops - 4 pieces each
top•backing
(print)
(batting)
(lightweight interfacing)

7 [2¾"]

2.8 [1⅛"]

● Instructions

1　Cut out each of the bag pieces referring to the template/pattern and dimensional diagram. Make the lower bag sections. Trace the appliqué design directly onto the top front and back of the lower bag section using a marking pencil. Trace and cut out the appliqué patterns, adding specified seam allowance*.

2　Use a 0.6 cm [¼"] bias tape maker to make several different colors of bias tape (0.3 cm [⅛"] finished) for the stalks and stems (see p. 21, Basics 4, 5).

3　Referring to Fig. 1, pin the bias tape for the stalks and stems in place; blindstitch them to the top (see p. 27, Akebia vines).

4　Appliqué the leaves and olives along the stems (Fig. 1).

5　With wrong sides together, layer the top and backing with batting in between; baste. Quilt the background as desired; quilt the veins in each of the leaves. Remove all of the basting stitches, except the basting around the edges.

6　Draw the finished sewing line of the bag outline on the backing of the bag front and bag back and sew the darts that are marked. With right sides together, pin the bag front and back in place and sew the side seams together (Fig. 2).

7　Trim the seam allowances down to 0.7 cm [¼"]. Make a 2.5 × 85 cm [1" × 33½"] bias binding from the backing fabric and bind the side seams; blindstitch down (Fig. 3).

8　To make the upper bag top sections, trace the appliqué design directly onto the top front and back of the upper bag section using a marking pencil. Trace and cut out the appliqué patterns, adding specified seam allowance*. Appliqué the stems, fruit and leaves to the upper bag section, leaving those appliqués that need to be attached to the lower bag section until later (Fig. 4).

9　With wrong sides together, layer the top and facing (muslin) with batting in between; baste. Quilt the background as desired; quilt the veins in each of the leaves. Remove all of the basting stitches, except the basting around the edges.

10　Make the handle loops by referring to Fig. 5; baste them in position on the upper bag section as shown (Fig. 6).

11　Cut 2 upper bag sections from the green print (facing) and fuse the lightweight interfacing to the wrong side. With right sides together, place the facing against the quilted upper bag section; and sew between markings. Snip into the curves and turn right side out; press (Fig. 7).

12　Cut 4 upper bag sections from the heavyweight interfacing. Position 1 side of the magnetic closure in place on the non-fusible side of the interfacing; spray the second piece of interfacing with spray adhesive on the non-fusible side. Press the 2 pieces together, sandwiching the magnetic closure between; stitch around the magnet to secure in place. Repeat for the other side with the remaining interfacing and magnetic closure. *Make sure the fusible side is facing out on both sides (Fig. 8).

13　With right sides together, pin the upper bag section to the lower bag section and sew between markings, being careful not to catch the facing in the stitching. Trim the seam allowance down to 0.7 [¼"]. Turn right side out. Insert the heavyweight interfacing pieces into each side of the upper bag sections. Fold under the seam allowance on the facing; cover the stitching and blindstitch down (Fig. 9).

14　Finish appliquéing the stems, fruit and leaves from the upper bag onto the lower bag sections. Following instructions for the heavyweight fusible interfacing, iron the upper bag sections to fuse the interfacing to the fabric on both sides (Fig. 10).

◆ Fig. 1

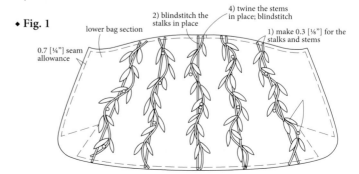

◆ Fig. 2

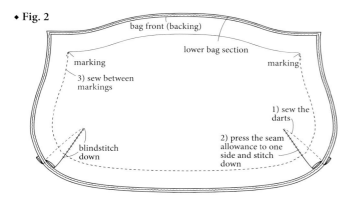

bag front (backing)

lower bag section

marking   marking

3) sew between markings

1) sew the darts

2) press the seam allowance to one side and stitch down

blindstitch down

◆ Fig. 3

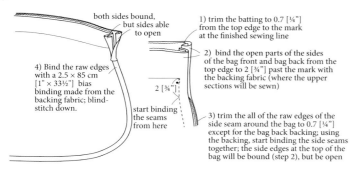

both sides bound, but sides able to open

4) Bind the raw edges with a 2.5 × 85 cm [1" × 33½"] bias binding made from the backing fabric; blind-stitch down.

1) trim the batting to 0.7 [¼"] from the top edge to the mark at the finished sewing line

2) bind the open parts of the sides of the bag front and bag back from the top edge to 2 [¾"] past the mark with the backing fabric (where the upper sections will be sewn)

2 [¾"]

start binding the seams from here

3) trim the all of the raw edges of the side seam around the bag to 0.7 [¼"] except for the bag back backing; using the backing, start binding the side seams together; the side edges at the top of the bag will be bound (step 2), but be open

◆ Fig. 4

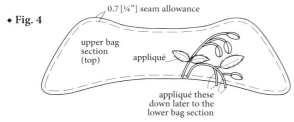

0.7 [¼"] seam allowance

upper bag section (top)

appliqué

appliqué these down later to the lower bag section

◆ Fig. 5

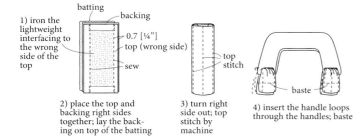

batting   backing

1) iron the lightweight interfacing to the wrong side of the top

0.7 [¼"]

top (wrong side)

sew

top stitch

baste

2) place the top and backing right sides together; lay the backing on top of the batting

3) turn right side out; top stitch by machine

4) insert the handle loops through the handles; baste

◆ Fig. 6

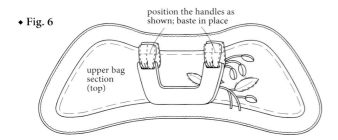

position the handles as shown; baste in place

upper bag section (top)

◆ Fig. 7

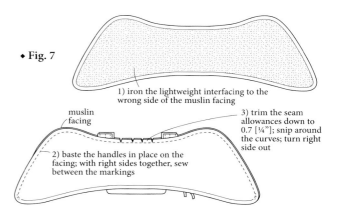

1) iron the lightweight interfacing to the wrong side of the muslin facing

muslin facing

3) trim the seam allowances down to 0.7 [¼"]; snip around the curves; turn right side out

2) baste the handles in place on the facing; with right sides together, sew between the markings

◆ Fig. 8

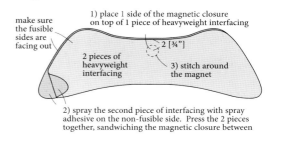

make sure the fusible sides are facing out

1) place 1 side of the magnetic closure on top of 1 piece of heavyweight interfacing

2 [¾"]

2 pieces of heavyweight interfacing

3) stitch around the magnet

2) spray the second piece of interfacing with spray adhesive on the non-fusible side. Press the 2 pieces together, sandwiching the magnetic closure between

◆ Fig. 9

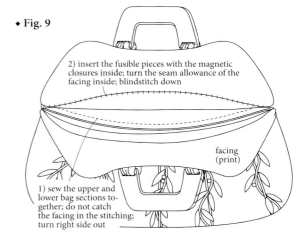

2) insert the fusible pieces with the magnetic closures inside; turn the seam allowance of the facing inside; blindstitch down

facing (print)

1) sew the upper and lower bag sections together; do not catch the facing in the stitching; turn right side out

◆ Fig. 10

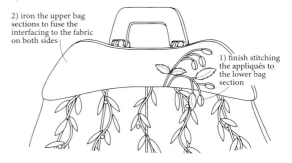

2) iron the upper bag sections to fuse the interfacing to the fabric on both sides

1) finish stitching the appliqués to the lower bag section

----- shown on p. 54

Shepherd's Purse Handbag

* Finished Measurements:
22 × 25 cm [8⅝" × 9¾"]; 4 cm [1½"] bottom
* The full-size template/pattern can be found on
Sides B and C of the pattern sheet inserts.

● Materials

Cottons
    Beige homespun - 25 × 31 cm [9¾" × 12¼"] (bag front top)
    Beige print - 25 × 31 cm [9¾" × 12¼"] (bag back top)
    Dk brown homespun - 15 × 15 cm [6¾" × 6¾"] (opening)
    Brown homespun - 6 × 28 cm [2⅜" × 11"] (bottom)
    Beige homespun - 110 × 30 cm [43¼" × 11¾"] (backing, bias binding)
    Assorted fat quarters or scraps (appliqué)
Batting - 90 × 30 cm [35⅜" × 11¾"]
Fusible interfacing - 10 × 26 cm [4" × 10¼"]
Embroidery thread - moss green, dk green, brown
Cotton or linen woven webbing - 2 × 55 cm [¾" × 21⅝"] (handle strap)
Rick rack trim (beige) - 30 cm [11¾"] (decoration on handle strap)

● Instructions

1 Cut out each of the bag pieces referring to the template/pattern and dimensional diagram. The design is the same as shown on p. 19. Trace the appliqué design directly onto the top front using a marking pencil. Trace and cut out the appliqué patterns, adding specified seam allowance*.
2 Place the bag front top and backing with right sides together and lay on top of the batting with the wrong side of the backing facing the batting. Machine sew the half-circle bag opening area only (Fig. 1). Repeat for the bag back.
3 Make several snips in the seam allowance along the curve and turn both pieces right side out; press. Top stitch along the edge of the half-circle opening. Quilt both the bag front and back (Fig. 2).
4 Refer to Fig. 3 to make the bottom of the bag.
5 With right sides together and matching edges, sew both the bag front and bag back to the bottom between marks (Fig. 4). Trim the top and batting down to 0.7 [¼"], leaving the backing. Use the backing to bind the raw edges of the bottom seams (Fig. 5).
6 With right sides of the bag front and bag back together, sew the side seams. Trim the top and batting down to 0.7 [¼"], leaving the backing. Press the seam allowances to one side and use the backing to bind the raw edges of the side seams (Fig. 5). Make a 2.5 × 12 cm [1" ×4¾"] piece of bias binding out of the backing fabric. Cut into 2 lengths of 6 cm [2⅜"] each. Bind the 2 short ends of the bag bottom with the bias binding; press toward the bottom and blindstitch (Fig. 5). Refer to the Cow Parsnip Handbag, p. 48, for detailed directions. Turn the bag right side out.
7 Fuse the 2 pieces of interfacing to the wrong side of the 2 pieces of the opening fabric. Referring to Fig. 6, with right sides together, sew the opening fabric pieces to the bag sides along the top. Trim the backing and batting down to 0.7 [¼"]. Fold the opening fabric up and press the seam allowances under 0.7 [¼"].
8 Make the handle strap referring to Fig. 7.
9 Turn the bag inside out. With the handle strap wrong side out, align against the opening fabric. Fold the opening fabric over the strap on both sides; pin in place. Blindstitch down to the backing. Machine quilt across the opening as shown or as desired (Fig. 8). Turn the bag right side out to complete the bag.

● Dimensional Diagram

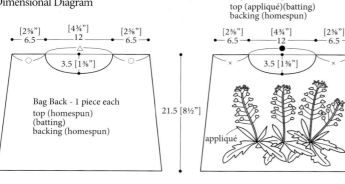

Bag Back - 1 piece each
top (homespun)
(batting)
backing (homespun)

[2⅝"] 6.5　[4¾"] 12　[2⅝"] 6.5

3.5 [1⅜"]

21.5 [8½"]

28.5 [11¼"]

Bag Front - 1 piece each
top (appliqué)(batting)
backing (homespun)

[2⅝"] 6.5　[4¾"] 12　[2⅝"] 6.5

3.5 [1⅜"]

appliqué

28.5 [11¼"]

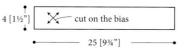

Bottom - 1 piece each
top (homespun)(batting)
backing (homespun)(interfacing)

4 [1½"]　cut on the bias

25 [9¾"]

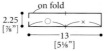

Opening Fabric - 2 pieces each
(homespun) (interfacing)

on fold

2.25 [⅞"]

13 [5⅛"]

* Seam allowances: do not add any seam allowance to the interfacing; add 0.7 cm [¼"] to all of the top pieces, and the opening piece; 3 cm [1¼"] to all other pieces.

◆ Fig. 1

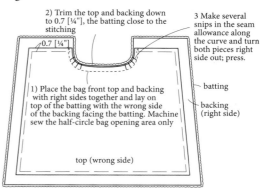

2) Trim the top and backing down to 0.7 [¼"], the batting close to the stitching

0.7 [¼"]

3 Make several snips in the seam allowance along the curve and turn both pieces right side out; press.

batting

backing (right side)

1) Place the bag front top and backing with right sides together and lay on top of the batting with the wrong side of the backing facing the batting. Machine sew the half-circle bag opening area only

top (wrong side)

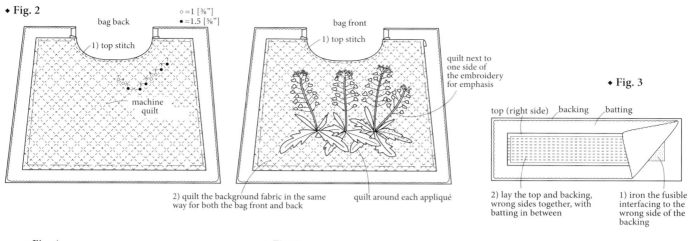

◆ Fig. 2

bag back

○ =1 [⅜"]
● =1.5 [⅝"]

1) top stitch

machine quilt

2) quilt the background fabric in the same way for both the bag front and back

bag front

1) top stitch

quilt next to one side of the embroidery for emphasis

quilt around each appliqué

◆ Fig. 3

top (right side)   backing   batting

2) lay the top and backing, wrong sides together, with batting in between

1) iron the fusible interfacing to the wrong side of the backing

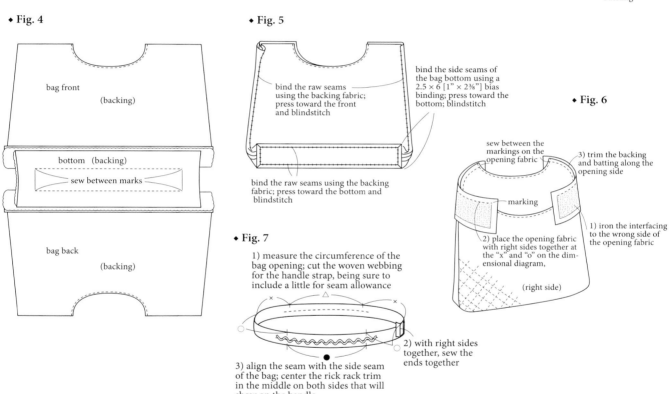

◆ Fig. 4

bag front
(backing)

bottom (backing)

sew between marks

bag back

(backing)

◆ Fig. 5

bind the raw seams using the backing fabric; press toward the front and blindstitch

bind the side seams of the bag bottom using a 2.5 × 6 [1" × 2⅜"] bias binding; press toward the bottom; blindstitch

bind the raw seams using the backing fabric; press toward the bottom and blindstitch

◆ Fig. 6

sew between the markings on the opening fabric

3) trim the backing and batting along the opening side

marking

2) place the opening fabric with right sides together at the "x" and "o" on the dimensional diagram,

1) iron the interfacing to the wrong side of the opening fabric

(right side)

◆ Fig. 7

1) measure the circumference of the bag opening; cut the woven webbing for the handle strap, being sure to include a little for seam allowance

2) with right sides together, sew the ends together

3) align the seam with the side seam of the bag; center the rick rack trim in the middle on both sides that will show on the handle

◆ Fig. 8

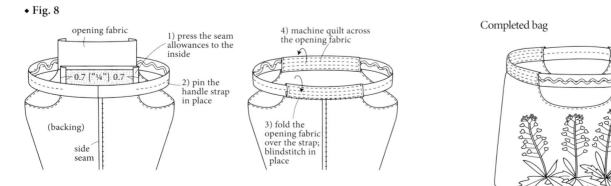

opening fabric

1) press the seam allowances to the inside

0.7 ["¼"] 0.7

2) pin the handle strap in place

(backing)

side seam

4) machine quilt across the opening fabric

3) fold the opening fabric over the strap; blindstitch in place

Completed bag

----- shown on p. 55

Spades & Clubs Messenger Bag

✴ Finished Measurements:
21.7 × 26 cm [8½" × 10¼"]; 4 cm [1½"] gusset
✴ The full-size template/pattern can be found on Side D of the pattern sheet inserts.

● Materials

Cottons

Dk brown homespun - 60 × 60 cm [23⅝" × 23⅝"] (top, magnetic closure covering)
Beige homespun - 27 × 18 cm [10⅝" × 7⅛"] (flap top a)
Lt pink print - 27 × 6 cm [10⅝" × 2⅜"] (flap top b)
Beige homespun - 27 × 7 cm [10⅝" × 2¾"] (flap top c)
Dk brown homespun - 110 × 65 cm [43¼" × 25⅝"] (all lining, flap back, zipper facing, magnetic closure covering)
Print - 60 × 60 cm [23⅝" × 23⅝"] (back accent, D ring loop, bias binding for the flap)
Grey homespun - 60 × 60 cm [23⅝" × 23⅝"] (bias binding for the bag opening)
Assorted fat quarters or scraps (appliqué)

● Dimensional Diagram

Back Accent - 1 piece each (print) (interfacing)

3 [1¼"]

← 26 [10¼"] →

0.7 [¼"]

binding (homespun)

Bag Front•Bag Back - 1 piece each
top (homespun) (batting)
lining (homespun) (interfacing)

21 [8¼"]

Bag Front Magnetic closure

center point   5 [2"]

← 26 [10¼"] →

Gusset - 1 piece each
top (homespun) (batting)
lining (homespun) (interfacing)

4 [1½"]

✕ cut the top on the bias

← 66 [26"] →

✴ Seam allowances: do not add any seam allowance to the interfacing; add 3 cm [1¼"] to the batting, all the lining; 0.7 cm [¼"] to all other pieces.

Materials (continued)

Batting - 45 × 100 cm [17¾" × 39⅜"]
Fusible interfacing - 30 × 90 cm [11¾" × 35⅜"]
Embroidery thread - dk brown, medium brown, off-white
Magnetic closure - 1.5 cm [⅝"] 1 set
Metal hardware - 2 D-rings 2.2 cm [⅞"]
1 Pre-made cotton webbing shoulder strap for bags

● Instructions

1 Cut out each of the bag pieces referring to the template/pattern and dimensional diagram. Trace the appliqué design directly onto the flap top (a) using a marking pencil. Trace and cut out the appliqué patterns, adding specified seam allowance*. Finish the appliqué and add the embroidery. Sew flap top (a), (b) and (c) together. With wrong sides together, layer the pieced flap top and lining with batting in between; baste. Quilt as shown or as desired (Fig. 1).
2 Referring to Fig. 2 and Fig. 3, put the zipper in the flap.
3 Make the back section of the flap (Fig. 4). With wrong sides together, baste the pieced flap and back section together around the edges. Measure around the flap to calculate the length; make 3.5 cm [1⅜"] wide bias binding. Bind the raw edges with the binding (Fig. 5).
4 Make the bag front, bag back and gusset. For each section, with wrong sides together, layer the top and lining with batting in between; baste. Quilt as shown or as desired (Fig. 6 and Fig. 7).
5 Refer to Fig. 8 to make the loops for the D-rings. Sew them to the gusset.
6 Sew the finished flap to the bag back referring to Fig. 9. Cover the seam with the back accent and top stitch in place.
7 Sew the gusset to the bag front and bag back. Trim the seam allowances for the top and batting to 0.7 cm [¼"]. Bind the seam with the lining fabric. Measure around the bag opening to calculate the circumference; make 3.5 cm [1⅜"] wide bias binding. Bind the raw edges with the binding (Fig. 10). Attach the shoulder strap to complete the messenger bag.

Flap Front - 1 piece each
top (print) (homespun) (batting)
lining (homespun)

[1½"] [1¾"]

4   4.5

binding (print)

a   b   c

appliqué

13 [5⅛"]

insert zipper here

attach zipper facing here

1 [⅜"]

← 24.5 [9⅝"] →

0.7 [¼"]   0.7 [¼"]

center point

Flap Back (homespun) - 2 pieces
(interfacing) - 1 piece

25 [9¾"]

Magnetic closure

center point   2 [¾"]

0.7 [¼"]

← 24.5 [9⅝"] →

Zipper Facing - 1 piece each
(homespun)
(interfacing)

2 [¾"]

cut down the center

stay stitch around the slit

iron on the interfacing

18 [7⅛"]

1 [⅜"]

4 [1½"]   2 [¾"]

D-ring Loops - 2 pieces each
top•lining (print)
(interfacing)

3.5 [1⅜"]

2.5 [1"]

3   Fabric to cover the magnetic closures (homespun) 2 pieces
[1¼"]

◆ Fig. 1

Double Lazy Daisy Stitch

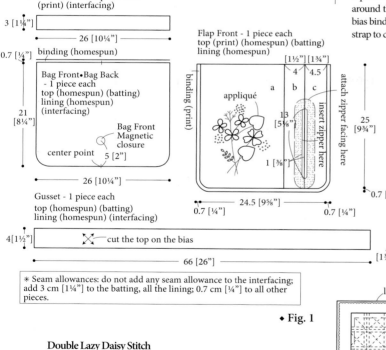

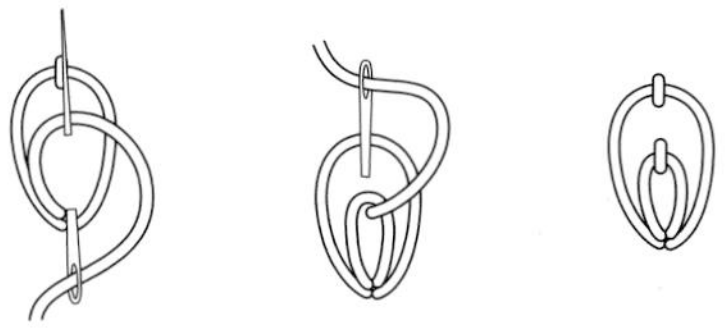

lining   batting

quilt, following the pattern on the fabric

2) with wrong sides together, layer the top and lining of the flap front, with batting in between; baste; quilt everywhere except where the zipper will be inserted

1) piece the flap top; add the appliqué and embroidery

quilt around the appliqué and embroidery

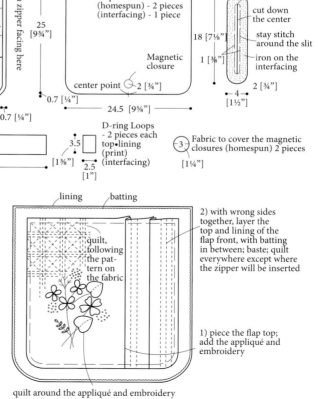

◆ Fig. 2

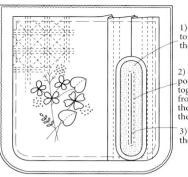

1) iron the interfacing to the wrong side of the zipper facing

2) place the facing in position, with right sides together, against the flap front top; stitch around the center cutting line for the slit

3) carefully cut down the center slit

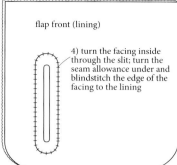

flap front (lining)

4) turn the facing inside through the slit; turn the seam allowance under and blindstitch the edge of the facing to the lining

◆ Fig. 3

2) finish the quilting

sew in the zipper

◆ Fig. 4

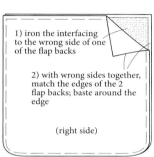

1) iron the interfacing to the wrong side of one of the flap backs

2) with wrong sides together, match the edges of the 2 flap backs; baste around the edge

(right side)

◆ Fig. 5

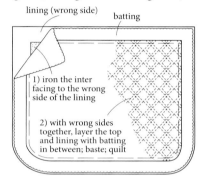

flap back   flap front (right side)

1) place the wrong sides of the flap front and flap back together

2) make a 3.5 × 80 [1⅜" × 31½"] bias binding; lay it, with right side together and edges matching, on the perimeter of the flap front

3) bind the raw edges with the bias binding; blindstitch down on the flap back

◆ Fig. 6 - (for Bag Front and Bag Back)

lining (wrong side)   batting

1) iron the inter facing to the wrong side of the lining

2) with wrong sides together, layer the top and lining with batting in between; baste; quilt

◆ Fig. 7 - Gusset

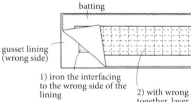

batting

gusset lining (wrong side)

1) iron the interfacing to the wrong side of the lining

2) with wrong sides together, layer the top and lining with batting in between; baste; quilt

◆ Fig. 8

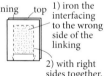

lining   top

1) iron the interfacing to the wrong side of the linking

2) with right sides together, sew the top and lining, leaving an opening

3) turn right side out and topstitch

4) trim the seam allowance

0.7 [¼"]

2.5

5) fold the seam allowances under and place the handle loop in position at the end of the gusset; blindstitch down

3

6) feed the handle loop through the D-ring; machine stitch down

◆ Fig. 9

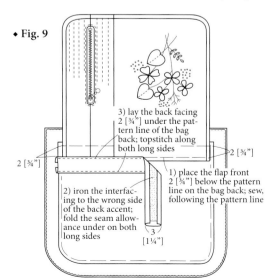

3) lay the back facing 2 [¾"] under the pattern line of the bag back; topstitch along both long sides

2 [¾"]

2 [¾"]

1) place the flap front 2 [¾"] below the pattern line on the bag back; sew, following the pattern line

2) iron the interfacing to the wrong side of the back accent; fold the seam allowance under on both long sides

3 [1¼"]

◆ Fig. 10

4) cover the magnetic closure with the fabric circle; blindstitch in place to the flap back

3) make a 3.5 × 64 [1⅜" × 25⅛"] bias binding; lay it, with right side together and edges matching, on the perimeter of the flap front

2) sew the bag back (with the flap attached) to the gusset; bind the seam allowance with the lining from the gusset; blindstitch down

0.7 [¼"] wide binding

1) sew the bag front to the gusset with right sides together; use the lining fabric from the gusset to bind the seams; blindstitch down

5) cover the magnetic closure with the fabric circle; blindstitch in place to the bag front

91

----- shown on p. 56

Fennel Mini Pouch

∗ Finished Measurements:
18.5 [7¼"]; 3 cm [1¼"] gusset
∗ The template/pattern can be found below.

● Materials

Cottons
    Dk brown print - 30 × 40 cm [11¾" × 15¾"] (bag and gusset top)
    Beige homespun - 110 × 40 cm [43¼" × 15¾"] (bag and gusset backing, bias binding for inner seams)
    Green print - (appliqué)
Batting - 35 × 60 cm [13¾" × 23⅝"]
Fusible interfacing - 5 × 32 cm [2" × 12⅝"]
Leather handles - 1 pair
1 Zipper (dk brown) - 15 cm [6¾"] long
1 Bead - optional (zipper pull)
Waxed cord - 12.5 cm [5"] (zipper pull)
4 Buttons - 1.1 cm [½"]
Embroidery thread - 3 shades of green, olive

● Instructions

1 Cut out each of the bag pieces referring to the template/pattern and dimensional diagram. Trace the appliqué design directly onto the top of the 4 sections (2 each of the right and left patterns) using a marking pencil. Trace and cut out the appliqué patterns, adding specified seam allowance∗.   Finish the appliqué and add the embroidery.   With wrong sides together, layer the top and backing with batting in between; baste. Quilt as shown or as desired (Fig. 1).
2 With right sides together and aligning marks, sew one left section and one right section together along the center seam. Trim the top and batting down to 0.7 cm [¼"]; use the backing to bind the raw edges (Fig. 2).
3 Refer to Fig. 3 and Fig. 4 to make both the zipper opening and the gusset.
4 With right sides together, sew the ends of the gusset to the ends of the zipper opening to form a circle. In the same way as above, trim the seam allowance and use the backing from the gusset to bind the raw edges along the seams (Fig. 5).
5 With right sides together, sew both the front and back sections of the bag to the zipper opening/gusset, matching marks and edges. Make a 2.5 × 52 cm [1" × 20½"] bias binding out of the backing fabric. For both sides, lay the bias binding against the gusset and zipper opening backing, matching the edges and sew along the seam line. Trim the seam allowance down to 0.7 cm [¼"]; fold the bias binding over the raw edges; press toward the bag backing and blindstitch down (Fig. 6).
6 Turn the bag right side out and attach the handles. To create the zipper pull, thread the waxed cord through the bead and zipper clasp; knot the ends to secure (Fig. 7).

● Dimensional Diagram

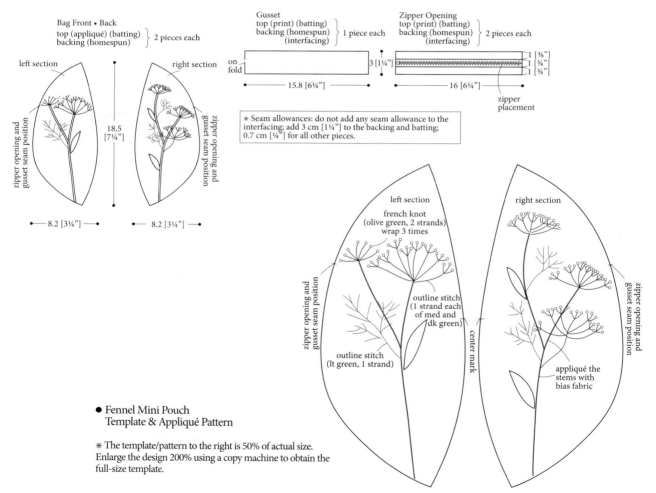

Bag Front • Back
top (appliqué) (batting)
backing (homespun) } 2 pieces each

left section

right section

zipper opening and gusset seam position

zipper opening and gusset seam position

18.5 [7¼"]

8.2 [3¼"]

8.2 [3¼"]

Gusset
top (print) (batting)
backing (homespun)
(interfacing) } 1 piece each

on fold

15.8 [6¼"]

3 [1¼"]

Zipper Opening
top (print) (batting)
backing (homespun)
(interfacing) } 2 pieces each

1 [⅜"]
1 [⅜"]
1 [⅜"]

16 [6¼"]

zipper placement

∗ Seam allowances: do not add any seam allowance to the interfacing; add 3 cm [1¼"] to the backing and batting; 0.7 cm [¼"] for all other pieces.

left section

french knot
(olive green, 2 strands)
wrap 3 times

outline stitch
(1 strand each
of med and
dk green)

outline stitch
(lt green, 1 strand)

zipper opening and gusset seam position

center mark

right section

appliqué the stems with bias fabric

zipper opening and gusset seam position

● Fennel Mini Pouch
    Template & Appliqué Pattern

∗ The template/pattern to the right is 50% of actual size.
Enlarge the design 200% using a copy machine to obtain the full-size template.

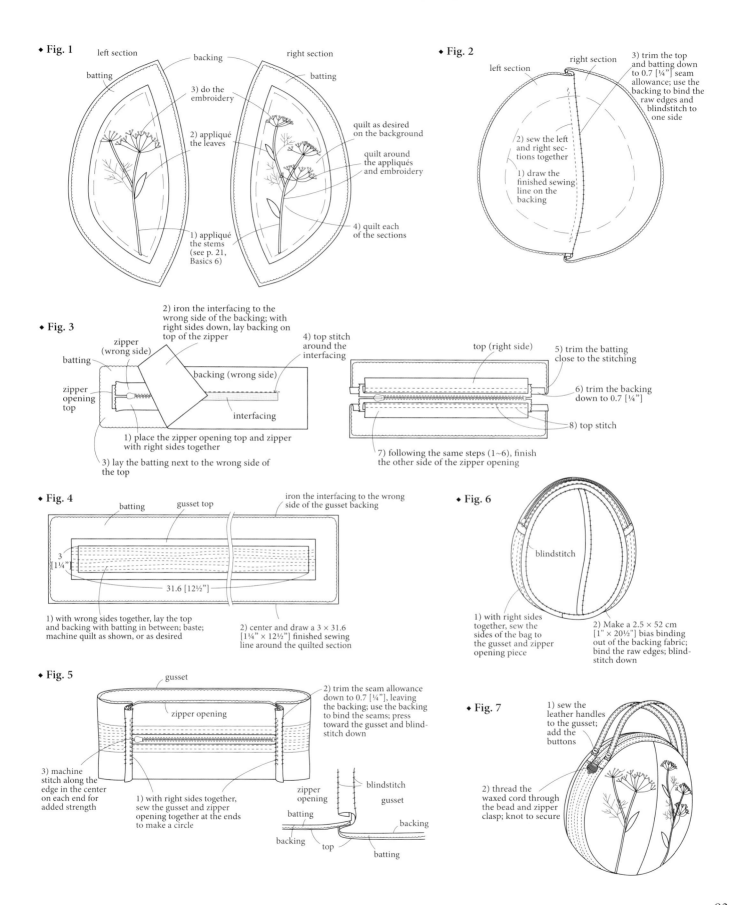

◆ **Fig. 1**

left section
batting
backing
right section
batting

3) do the embroidery

quilt as desired on the background

2) appliqué the leaves

quilt around the appliqués and embroidery

1) appliqué the stems (see p. 21, Basics 6)

4) quilt each of the sections

◆ **Fig. 2**

left section
right section

3) trim the top and batting down to 0.7 [¼"] seam allowance; use the backing to bind the raw edges and blindstitch to one side

2) sew the left and right sections together

1) draw the finished sewing line on the backing

◆ **Fig. 3**

2) iron the interfacing to the wrong side of the backing; with right sides down, lay backing on top of the zipper

zipper (wrong side)

4) top stitch around the interfacing

batting

backing (wrong side)

zipper opening top

interfacing

1) place the zipper opening top and zipper with right sides together

3) lay the batting next to the wrong side of the top

top (right side)

5) trim the batting close to the stitching

6) trim the backing down to 0.7 [¼"]

8) top stitch

7) following the same steps (1~6), finish the other side of the zipper opening

◆ **Fig. 4**

batting
gusset top
iron the interfacing to the wrong side of the gusset backing

3 [1¼"]

31.6 [12½"]

1) with wrong sides together, lay the top and backing with batting in between; baste; machine quilt as shown, or as desired

2) center and draw a 3 × 31.6 [1¼" × 12½"] finished sewing line around the quilted section

◆ **Fig. 5**

gusset

2) trim the seam allowance down to 0.7 [¼"], leaving the backing; use the backing to bind the seams; press toward the gusset and blindstitch down

zipper opening

3) machine stitch along the edge in the center on each end for added strength

1) with right sides together, sew the gusset and zipper opening together at the ends to make a circle

blindstitch

zipper opening

gusset

batting

backing

backing

top

batting

◆ **Fig. 6**

blindstitch

1) with right sides together, sew the sides of the bag to the gusset and zipper opening piece

2) Make a 2.5 × 52 cm [1" × 20½"] bias binding out of the backing fabric; bind the raw edges; blind-stitch down

◆ **Fig. 7**

1) sew the leather handles to the gusset; add the buttons

2) thread the waxed cord through the bead and zipper clasp; knot to secure

----- shown on p. 57

Nigella Bag

* Finished Measurements:
  22.5 × 18.5 [8⅞" × 7¼"]; 5 cm [2"] gusset
* The full-size template/pattern can be found on
  Side D of the pattern sheet inserts.

● Materials

Cottons

Beige print - 25 × 21 cm [9¾" × 8¼"] (bag front top)
Beige homespun - 25 × 21 cm [9¾" × 8¼"] (bag back top)
Beige homespun - 40 × 40 cm [15¾" × 15¾"] (zipper opening and gusset top)
Beige homespun - 110 × 50 cm [43¼" × 19¾"] (backing, bias binding for inner seams)
Brown homespun - 13 × 7 cm [5⅛" × 2¾"] (zipper tabs)
Assorted fat quarters or scraps (appliqué)
Batting - 100 × 30 cm [39⅜" × 11¾"]
Fusible interfacing - 31 × 41 cm [12¼" × 16⅛"]
Handles - 1 pair
1 Zipper (beige) - 23 cm [9"] long
2 Beads - optional (zipper pull)
Waxed cord (green) - 20 cm [7⅞"] (zipper pull)
Embroidery thread - green, yellow-green, purple

● Instructions

1 Cut out each of the bag pieces referring to the template/pattern and dimensional diagram. Trace the appliqué design directly onto the front top using a marking pencil. Trace and cut out the appliqué patterns, adding specified seam allowance*. Finish the appliqué and add the embroidery. With wrong sides together, layer the front top and backing with batting in between; baste. Quilt as shown or as desired (Fig. 1).

2 Iron the fusible interfacing to the wrong side of the backing of the bag back. With wrong sides together, layer the back top and backing with batting in between; baste. Quilt as shown or as desired (Fig. 1).

3 Make the zipper tabs (Fig. 2).

4 Refer to p. 92, 93 to make the zipper opening in the same way as for the Fennel Mini Pouch. Baste the 2 zipper tabs to either end of the zipper opening as shown (Fig. 3).

5 Make the gusset by referring to Fig. 4.

6 With right sides together, sew the ends of the gusset to the ends of the zipper opening to form a circle. Trim the seam allowance from the top and batting down to 0.7 cm [¼"] and use the backing from the gusset to bind the raw edges along the seams (Fig. 5).

7 Baste the handles, in position, to both the front and back bag sections. With right sides together, sew both the front and back sections of the bag to the zipper opening/gusset, matching marks and edges (Fig. 6).

8 Make a 2.5 × 65 cm [1" × 25⅝"] bias binding out of the backing fabric. With the bag inside out and for both the front and back, lay the bias binding, right sides together, against the gusset and zipper opening backing, matching the edges, and sew along the seam line. Trim the seam allowance for the top and batting down to 0.7 cm [¼"], fold the bias binding over the raw edges; press toward the bag backing and blindstitch down (see p. 93, Fig. 6 of the Fennel Mini Pouch).

9 Turn the bag right side out. To create the zipper pull, fold the waxed thread in half and thread it through the beads and zipper clasp; knot the ends to secure (Fig. 6).

● Dimensional Diagram

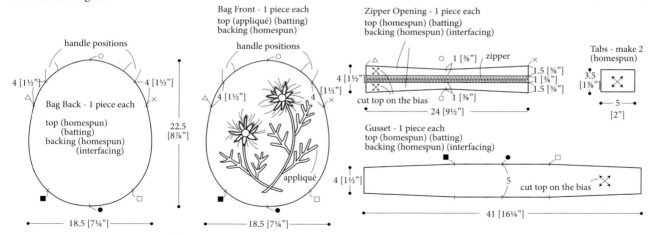

* Seam allowances: do not add any seam allowance to the interfacing; add 3 cm [1¼"] to the backing and batting; 0.7 cm [¼"] for all other pieces.

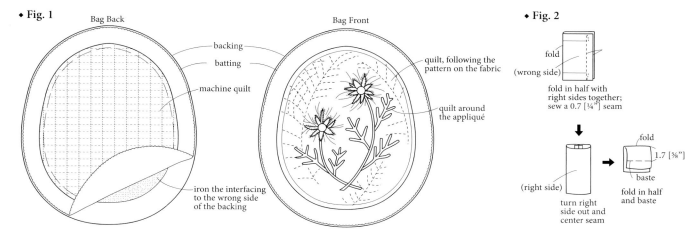

◆ Fig. 1

Bag Back

backing

batting

machine quilt

iron the interfacing to the wrong side of the backing

Bag Front

quilt, following the pattern on the fabric

quilt around the appliqué

◆ Fig. 2

fold

(wrong side)

fold in half with right sides together; sew a 0.7 [¼"] seam

(right side)

turn right side out and center seam

fold

1.7 [⅝"]

baste

fold in half and baste

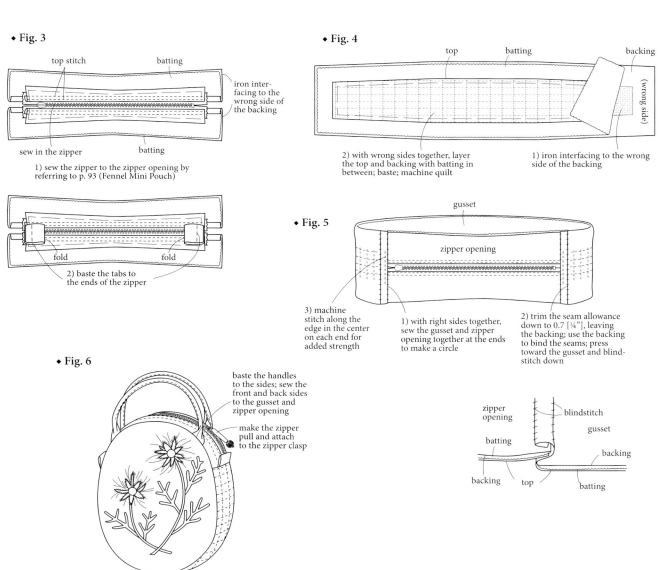

◆ Fig. 3

top stitch   batting

iron inter-facing to the wrong side of the backing

sew in the zipper   batting

1) sew the zipper to the zipper opening by referring to p. 93 (Fennel Mini Pouch)

fold   fold

2) baste the tabs to the ends of the zipper

◆ Fig. 4

top   batting   backing

(wrong side)

2) with wrong sides together, layer the top and backing with batting in between; baste; machine quilt

1) iron interfacing to the wrong side of the backing

◆ Fig. 5

gusset

zipper opening

3) machine stitch along the edge in the center on each end for added strength

1) with right sides together, sew the gusset and zipper opening together at the ends to make a circle

2) trim the seam allowance down to 0.7 [¼"], leaving the backing; use the backing to bind the seams; press toward the gusset and blind-stitch down

◆ Fig. 6

baste the handles to the sides; sew the front and back sides to the gusset and zipper opening

make the zipper pull and attach to the zipper clasp

zipper opening

blindstitch

gusset

batting

backing

backing   top   batting

----- shown on p. 58

Peas Shopping Bag

* Finished Measurements:
  43 × 31.5 [16⅞" × 12⅜"]
* The appliqué pattern can be found on
  Side A of the pattern sheet inserts.

● Materials

Cottons
  Beige homespun - 88 × 22 cm [34⅝" × 8⅝"] (bag fabric A)
  Green homespun - 88 × 13 cm [34⅝" × 5⅛"] (bag fabric B)
  Lt brown print - 88 × 35 cm [34⅝" × 13¾"] (lining)
  Assorted fat quarters or scraps (appliqué)
Embroidery thread - lt green, green, dk brown

● Dimensional Diagram

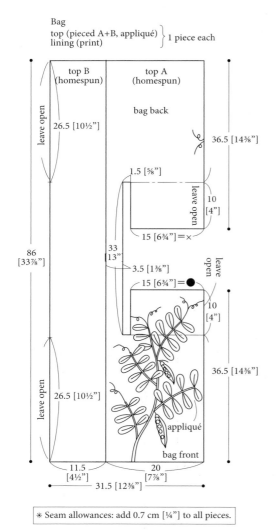

* Seam allowances: add 0.7 cm [¼"] to all pieces.

● Instructions

1 Cut out each of the bag pieces, except for the lining, referring to the template/pattern and dimensional diagram. The design is the alternate design shown on p. 17. Trace the appliqué design directly onto bag fabric A using a marking pencil. Trace and cut out the appliqué patterns, adding specified seam allowance*. Do the appliqué and embroidery, leaving the embroidery that wraps around to the back side. With right sides together, sew bag fabric A to bag fabric B. Press the seam allowance toward A; top stitch along the seam (Fig. 1). This becomes the top fabric.

2 Cut out the lining in one large piece the same size as the top. Fold the top fabric in half, with right sides together, and sew just along the top (shorter edge) between marks (Fig. 2). Fold and sew the lining as same as for the top so that when placed right sides together, the seams on the shorter edge line up.

3 Pin the top and lining with right sides together. Refer to Fig. 3 and 4 to cut the center slit and stay stitch around the opening.

4 Fold the top/lining piece in half, with right sides together; sew the side and bottom seams, leaving the opening area for turning (Fig. 5).

5 Turn the bag right side out through the opening, starting with the long side and adjust the shape. Turn the seam allowance under at the opening and blindstitch closed; top stitch along the edge (Fig. 6).

6 Finish the remaining embroidery on the back side (Fig. 7).

◆ **Fig. 1**

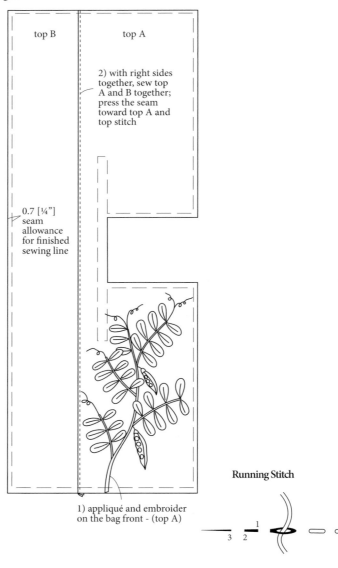

Running Stitch

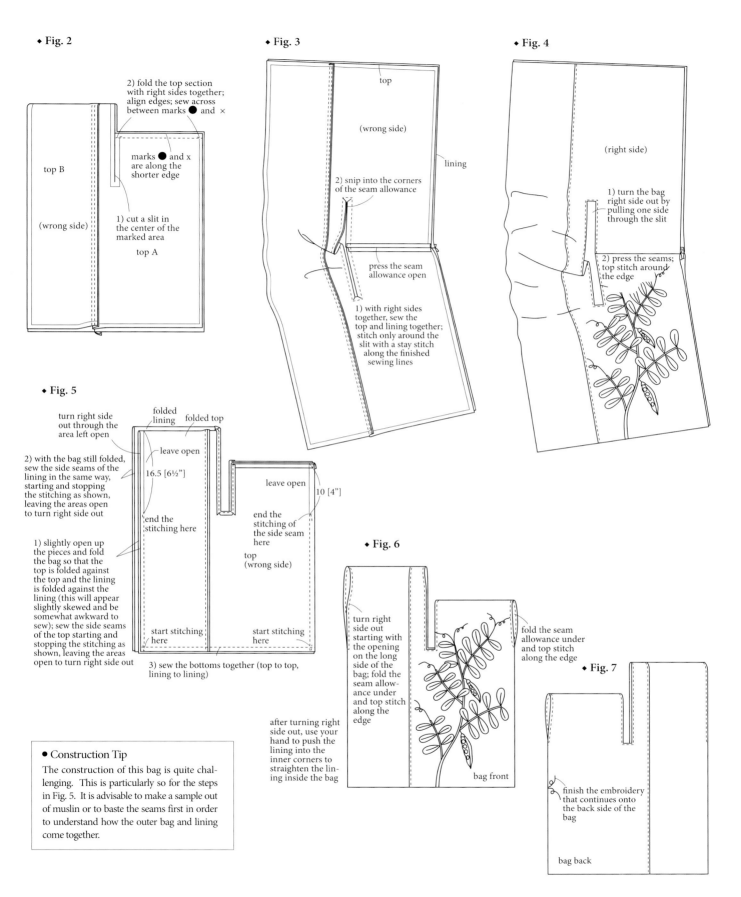

◆ Fig. 2

2) fold the top section with right sides together; align edges; sew across between marks ● and ×

marks ● and x are along the shorter edge

top B

(wrong side)

1) cut a slit in the center of the marked area

top A

◆ Fig. 3

top

(wrong side)

lining

2) snip into the corners of the seam allowance

press the seam allowance open

1) with right sides together, sew the top and lining together; stitch only around the slit with a stay stitch along the finished sewing lines

◆ Fig. 4

(right side)

1) turn the bag right side out by pulling one side through the slit

2) press the seams; top stitch around the edge

◆ Fig. 5

turn right side out through the area left open

folded lining

folded top

leave open

16.5 [6½"]

2) with the bag still folded, sew the side seams of the lining in the same way, starting and stopping the stitching as shown, leaving the areas open to turn right side out

end the stitching here

1) slightly open up the pieces and fold the bag so that the top is folded against the top and the lining is folded against the lining (this will appear slightly skewed and be somewhat awkward to sew); sew the side seams of the top starting and stopping the stitching as shown, leaving the areas open to turn right side out

leave open

10 [4"]

end the stitching of the side seam here

top (wrong side)

start stitching here

start stitching here

3) sew the bottoms together (top to top, lining to lining)

◆ Fig. 6

turn right side out starting with the opening on the long side of the bag; fold the seam allowance under and top stitch along the edge

after turning right side out, use your hand to push the lining into the inner corners to straighten the lining inside the bag

fold the seam allowance under and top stitch along the edge

bag front

◆ Fig. 7

finish the embroidery that continues onto the back side of the bag

bag back

● Construction Tip

The construction of this bag is quite challenging. This is particularly so for the steps in Fig. 5. It is advisable to make a sample out of muslin or to baste the seams first in order to understand how the outer bag and lining come together.

----- shown on p. 59

Wild Strawberry
Shoulder Bag

✴ Finished Measurements:
27.5 × 21 [10⅞" × 8¼"]
✴ The full-size template/pattern can be found
on Side D of the pattern sheet inserts.

● Materials

Cottons
Grey homespun - 110 × 40 cm [43¼" × 15¾"] (flap top, bag back top, shoulder strap)
Grey print - 35 × 30 cm [13¾" × 11¾"] (bag front top)
Dk blue homespun - 110 × 40 cm [43¼" × 15¾"] (flap lining, bag front lining, bag back lining)
Muslin - 35 × 60 cm [13¾" × 23⅝"] (facing)
Brown print - 3.5 × 160 cm [1⅜" × 63"] (bias binding)
4 Assorted fat quarters or scraps (appliqué)
Batting - 35 × 60 cm [13¾" × 23⅝"]
Woven cotton webbing - 110 × 3 cm [43¼" × 1¼"] (to go inside shoulder strap)
Fusible interfacing - 71 × 28 cm [28" × 11"]
Embroidery thread - black, mustard, 2 shades of brown, 3 shades of green

● Instructions

1 Cut out each of the bag pieces referring to the template/pattern and dimensional diagram. Trace the appliqué design directly onto the flap top using a marking pencil. Trace and cut out the appliqué patterns, adding specified seam allowance*. Finish the appliqué and add the embroidery. With wrong sides together, layer the flap top and facing with batting in between; baste. Quilt as shown or as desired. Sew the darts (Fig. 1).

2 Referring to Fig. 2, make the lining for the flap. Spray the wrong sides of the flap front and the flap back with spray adhesive; layer them, with wrong sides (facing) together, matching edges.

3 Make the shoulder strap by referring to Fig. 3.

4 Make both the bag back lining and the bag back top (Fig. 4). Baste the shoulder strap to the top of the back bag top (Fig. 5).

5 Referring to Fig. 5, layer the bag back top (right side up), the flap (appliquéd side down on bag back top) and the bag back lining (right side against the flap), matching edges and with shoulder strap sandwiched in between the bag back and flap layers. Sew across the straight edges, catching the shoulder strap ends. Flip the flap layer back over, spray the adhesive to the wrong side (facing) of the bag back top and the bag back lining, matching edges and press together (Fig. 6).

6 Make the bag front (Fig. 7). Turn it right side out, quilt as desired. Sew the darts and press toward the center (Fig. 8).

7 With the piece open (Fig. 8), lay the bag front on top of the bag back with wrong sides together, matching edges; pin. Sew the bag front to the bag back along the seams.

8 Make the bias binding and with right sides together, align it to the edges all the way around the bag body and flap. Stitch down. Trim the raw edges down to 0.7 cm [¼"], fold the bias binding over and bind the raw edges; blindstitch down to complete the bag (Fig. 8).

● Dimensional Diagram

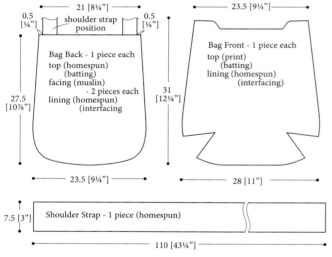

21 [8¼"]
0.5 [¼"]
shoulder strap position
0.5 [¼"]
Bag Back - 1 piece each
top (homespun)
(batting)
facing (muslin)
- 2 pieces each
lining (homespun)
(interfacing
27.5 [10⅞"]
23.5 [9¼"]

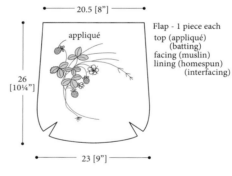

23.5 [9¼"]
Bag Front - 1 piece each
top (print)
(batting)
lining (homespun)
(interfacing)
31 [12¼"]
28 [11"]

20.5 [8"]
appliqué
Flap - 1 piece each
top (appliqué)
(batting)
facing (muslin)
lining (homespun)
(interfacing)
26 [10¼"]
23 [9"]

7.5 [3"]
Shoulder Strap - 1 piece (homespun)
110 [43¼"]

✴ Seam allowances: do not add any seam allowance to the interfacing; add 0.7 cm [¼"] to the top pieces; 3 cm [1¼"] to all other pieces.

◆ Fig. 1

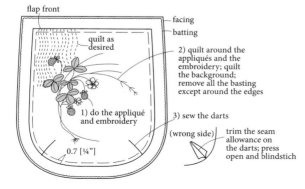

flap front
facing
batting
quilt as desired
2) quilt around the appliqués and the embroidery; quilt the background; remove all the basting except around the edges
1) do the appliqué and embroidery
3) sew the darts
0.7 [¼"]
(wrong side)
trim the seam allowance on the darts; press open and blindstich

◆ Fig. 2

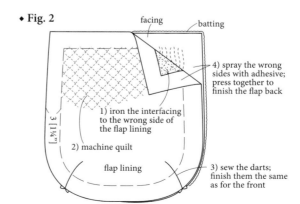

facing
batting
4) spray the wrong sides with adhesive; press together to finish the flap back
1) iron the interfacing to the wrong side of the flap lining
3 [1¼"]
2) machine quilt
flap lining
3) sew the darts; finish them the same as for the front

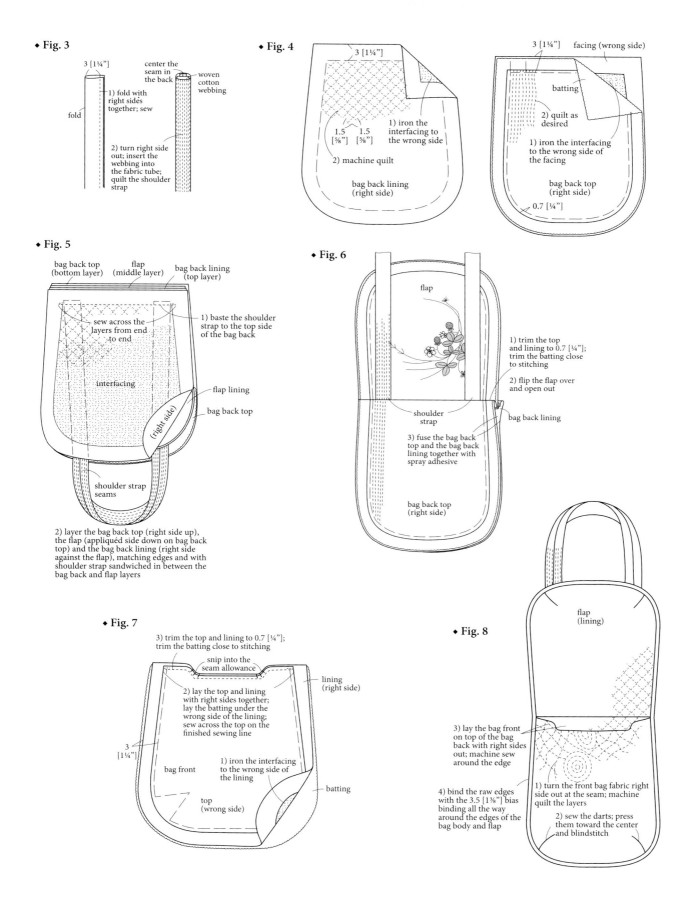

◆ Fig. 3

3 [1¼"]

fold

center the seam in the back

woven cotton webbing

1) fold with right sides together; sew

2) turn right side out; insert the webbing into the fabric tube; quilt the shoulder strap

◆ Fig. 4

3 [1¼"]

1.5 [⅝"] 1.5 [⅝"]

1) iron the interfacing to the wrong side

2) machine quilt

bag back lining (right side)

3 [1¼"] facing (wrong side)

batting

2) quilt as desired

1) iron the interfacing to the wrong side of the facing

bag back top (right side)

0.7 [¼"]

◆ Fig. 5

bag back top (bottom layer)   flap (middle layer)   bag back lining (top layer)

sew across the layers from end to end

interfacing

1) baste the shoulder strap to the top side of the bag back

flap lining

bag back top

(right side)

shoulder strap seams

2) layer the bag back top (right side up), the flap (appliquéd side down on bag back top) and the bag back lining (right side against the flap), matching edges and with shoulder strap sandwiched in between the bag back and flap layers

◆ Fig. 6

flap

1) trim the top and lining to 0.7 [¼"]; trim the batting close to stitching

2) flip the flap over and open out

shoulder strap

bag back lining

3) fuse the bag back top and the bag back lining together with spray adhesive

bag back top (right side)

◆ Fig. 7

3) trim the top and lining to 0.7 [¼"]; trim the batting close to stitching

snip into the seam allowance

lining (right side)

2) lay the top and lining with right sides together; lay the batting under the wrong side of the lining; sew across the top on the finished sewing line

3 [1¼"]

bag front

1) iron the interfacing to the wrong side of the lining

top (wrong side)

batting

◆ Fig. 8

flap (lining)

3) lay the bag front on top of the bag back with right sides out; machine sew around the edge

1) turn the front bag fabric right side out at the seam; machine quilt the layers

4) bind the raw edges with the 3.5 [1⅜"] bias binding all the way around the edges of the bag body and flap

2) sew the darts; press them toward the center and blindstitch

99

----- shown on p. 63

"Woods of Green" Wall Quilt

* Finished Measurements:
  201.4 × 179.4 cm [79⅜" × 70½"]
* The appliqué patterns can be found on Sides A and B of the pattern sheet inserts.

● Dimensional Diagram

● Materials

Cottons
  Homespun "Z" - 110 × 420 cm [43¼" × 4⅔ yds] (backing)
  Beige print - 110 × 210 cm [43¼" × 2⅓ yds] (borders)
  Dk brown print - 10 × 180 cm [4" × 2 yds] (ground appliqué)
  Brown print - 55 × 240 cm [21⅝" × 2⅔ yds] (tree appliqué))
  Moss green print - 35 × 210 cm [13¾" × 2⅓ yds] (tree appliqué))
  Deep brown print - 10 × 50 cm [4" × 19¾"] (tree appliqué)
  Homespun "Y" - 3.5 cm × 760 cm [1⅜" × 8⅓ yds or 300"] (bias binding)
  Assorted fat quarters or scraps (appliqué for border a)
Batting - 210 × 190 cm [2⅓ yds × 2¼ yd.]

In addition, 24 completed, appliquéd and embroidered blocks from the "Plants Through the Four Seasons" designs and patterns shown on p. 6~19.

Quilt - 1 of each
top (pieced top) (batting)
backing (homespun "Z")

binding (homespun "Y")

A = main pattern
B = alternate design

※ Seam allowances: add 0.3 cm [⅛"] to the appliqué pieces; 1 cm [⅜"] to all other pieces; prepare a 210 × 190 cm [82½" × 74½"] backing and batting

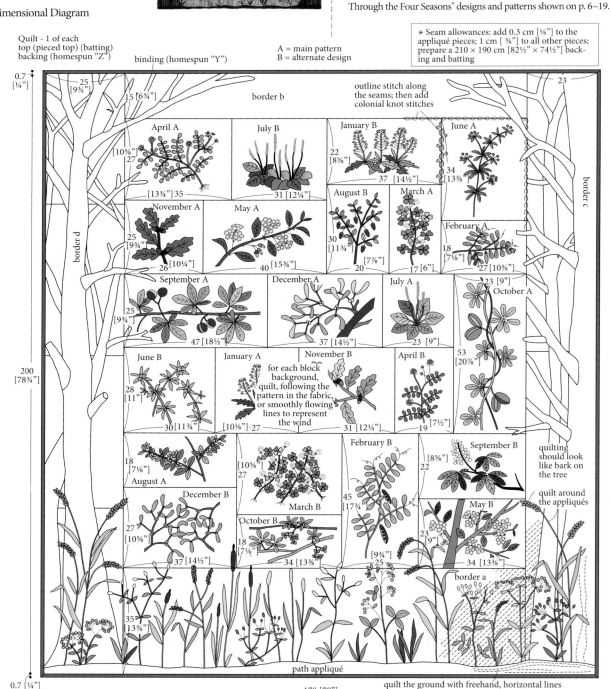

100

1 Piecing and Making the Blocks for the Center of the Quilt Top

Block Assembly

• Assembling the blocks into the quilt top is up to the individual, but they should be organized in such a way as to form 3 large horizontal sections that are the same width (see the dimensional diagram on p. 100). Use a design wall or the floor to place the blocks in position, and move them around until you find the overall composition that you find most pleasing. Once you have decided the block positions, decide how wide you want to make your borders to best balance the entire quilt visually.

Start by sewing the smaller blocks to each other to create larger block sections; continue this until you have 3 large horizontal sections of the same width. Sew the 3 sections together to form the center of the quilt.

Sewing Tips

• When piecing the blocks by hand, start 0.5 cm [¼"] in from the end (at the mark). Sew the seam with a running stitch, and do a single backstitch at the beginning and end to secure the stitches. Also take a single backstitch at any point where seams overlap, for stronger seams.

• After sewing the seams, trim the seam allowances down to 0.7 cm [¼"].

• Press the seam allowances to one side after sewing the blocks together. As there are no areas where seams of the blocks line up exactly, it doesn't matter to which side the seams are pressed.

April A   **July B**

November A   **May A**

(wrong side)

1 Make the first 4 blocks. With right sides together, pin April A (Lotus Flower) to July B (Plaintain) along the sides. Begin sewing 0.5 cm [¼"] in from the end, starting with a single backstitch, then continuing with a running stitch along the finished seam line.

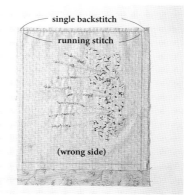
single backstitch
running stitch
(wrong side)

2 At 0.5 cm [¼"] from the end, run your fingers along the seam to even out the stitching so that the fabric is not being pulled and is smooth. Take a single backstitch to secure; knot and clip the thread.

3 Trim the seam allowances down to 0.7 cm [¼"].

4 If you've sewn the seams by hand, fold the seam allowance toward the block with the darker fabric and finger press it down approximately 0.1 cm [¹/₁₆"]. Use your fingernails for a crisp crease. Open up the pieces, right side up.

5 Next, sew together November A (Oak Leaves & Acorns) to May A (Mountain Cherry) following steps 1~4. Press the seam allowance toward the May A block.

single backstitch
sew

6 With right sides together, sew the 2 block sections together to create 1 large piece. If sewing by hand, remember to take a single backstitch at the ends and where any seams overlap. Press the seam allowances toward the bottom side. This set of 4 blocks becomes piece "Z".

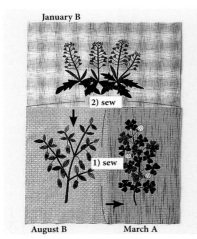

January B

2) sew

1) sew

August B   March A

7 With right sides together, sew August B (Wolfberry) to March A (Clover). Press the seam allowance toward the March A block. Sew the January B (Shepherd's Purse) block to the top of the section just completed. Press the seam allowance toward the bottom. This set of 3 blocks becomes piece "Y".

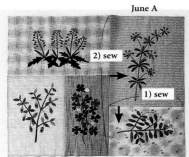

June A

2) sew

1) sew

February A

8 With right sides together, sew June A (Goose Grass) to February A (Peas). Sew this section to piece "Y" and press the seam allowance toward the peas. This set of blocks becomes piece "X".

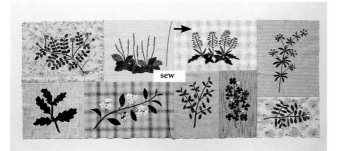

sew

9 Sew pieces "Z" and "X" together and press the seam toward piece "X". This completes the top large horizontal section of the quilt center.

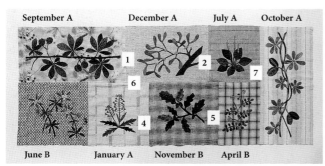

September A   December A   July A   October A

1

6

2

7

4

5

June B   January A   November B   April B

10 Begin making the middle horizontal section of the quilt center. Sew September A and December A together (1), followed by July A to December A. (2) Next, sew June B to January A (3), then, November B to January A (4), followed by April B to November B (5). Sew the top row to the bottom row (6). Finally, sew October A to the section (7). This completes the middle section.

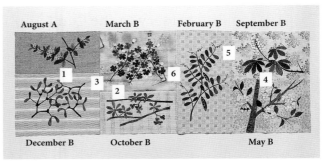

August A   March B   February B   September B

1

3

2

6

5

4

December B   October B   May B

11 Make the bottom horizontal section of the quilt center. Begin by sewing August A to December B (1), followed by March B to October B (2). Then sew those sections together (3). This set of blocks becomes piece "W". Next, sew September B to May B (4). Sew this section to February B (5). This set of blocks becomes piece "V". Sew piece "W" to piece "V" to create the bottom section of the quilt center.

sew

sew

12 With right sides together, sew the top section to the middle section. Press the seams toward the middle section. With right sides together, sew the bottom section to the middle section. Press the seams toward the bottom section. Press the quilt top. The piecing of the center section of the quilt top is complete.

2 Adding Embroidery to the Quilt Top

✳ Embroider over the seams between the blocks in the quilt center. Referring to the embroidery design on the template/pattern on Side A of the pattern sheet inserts, draw freehand along the seams with a marking pencil. Use the lines as a guide as you embroider. Add the colonial knot stitches freehand.

1 Hoop the quilt top, centering the seams. Using 2 strands of lt beige embroidery thread, outline stitch the design marked along the seams.

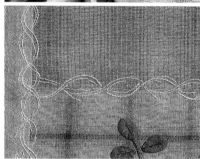

2 Using 3 strands of lt beige embroidery thread, embroider groupings of 4-5 colonial knot stitches to the left and right of the outline stitching as shown.

3 Outline stitch and add colonial knot stitches along each horizontal and vertical seam between the blocks. This completes the center section of the quilt top.

3 Finishing the Quilt Top

appliqué these down after the border is sewn to the quilt center

0.5 [¼"]

finished sewing line for ground appliqué

1 Trace the appliqué design, including the ground position, directly onto the front of border a, using a marking pencil. Trace and cut out the appliqué patterns, adding specified seam allowance*. Cut the stems out of 1.2 cm [½"] wide bias strips and draw a finished sewing line 0.3 [⅛"] from the end. Pin the stems to the border, with the end of the stems 0.5 cm [¼"] below the line drawn showing where the ground piece gets appliquéd. Start appliquéing from the bottom of each stem (referring to Basics 6 (p. 21). For every appliqué that overlaps onto the center of the quilt, leave the top 7~8 cm [7¾"~8⅛"] without stitching them, as they will be appliquéd down after the border is sewn to the quilt center. Appliqué the leaves, fruit and flowers for each design, turning the seam allowance under as you blindstitch each down to the border.

border d   border b   border c

border a

ground

2 Trace the tree appliqué design directly onto border b, c and d using a marking pencil. Trace and cut out the appliqué tree patterns, adding a 0.5 cm [¼"] seam allowance. Appliqué the branches and trunk of the tree. For any branches that overlap onto the quilt center or other border, stop stitching 2~3 cm [¾"~1¼"] from the edge and leave them loose. These will be stitched down after the borders are sewn on.

✻ Make border pieces c and d 202 cm [79½"] long by piecing together the beige print.

2) sew

3) sew

4 sew

1) sew

3 Sew the borders to the quilt center in the following order: a, b, c, and d. Press the seam allowances toward the borders.

4 Finish stitching down any appliqués that were left loose before the borders were sewn on. Pin the branches to the background, fold the seam allowances under while you blindstitch them down. Snip into the "v" of the seam allowance if necessary, to help with ease.

5 Blindstitch to the point just before the snipped area, use the tip of the needle to turn the seam allowance under while you sew.

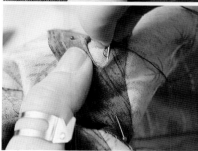

6 Once you make the snips in the seam allowance close to the finished sewing line, there will not be any fabric to fold under at the point. Take 3 tiny stitches at the inverted point to secure and continue to blindstitch around the appliqué.

8 Pin the appliqué piece for the ground in position at the bottom of border a, aligning the finished sewing line to the line drawn on the border with the marking pencil. Baste it in place below the finished sewing line. Snip, as needed, along the curving top of the piece to help with ease. Blindstitch it to the background, turning the seam allowance under as you go, making sure that the stem ends from the appliqués are covered by the ground appliqué. The quilt top is complete.

7 Pin the stems and flowers from border a that were left loose to the quilt center and borders c and d at the bottom. Finish stitching down any appliqués. Next, finish any embroidery that was left unfinished.

4 Layering and Basting the Quilt

Make the backing (see below ✳). Smooth out the backing fabric (wrong side up) on a flat surface and pin or tape to hold it taut. With the batting cut to the same size as the backing, lay it on top of the backing and re-pin or tape both layers to the flat surface. Center the quilt top on top of the layers and pin down. Starting in the center of the quilt top with a length of knotted thread, baste to the left edge. Backstitch at the end and knot the thread; cut it leaving a 2~3 cm [¾"~1½"]tail. Start again at the center and baste out to the right edge. Then baste vertically, top to bottom. Repeat this diagonally. No wide spaces should be left unbasted so that the layers do not shift during quilting.

✳ **Make the Backing**
Prepare a backing the size of 210 × 190 cm [82½" × 74½"]. You will need to sew 2 lengths of fabric together down the middle with a sewing machine or a running stitch, if sewing by hand. Press the seam allowance to one side.

5 Loading the Quilt onto a Quilting Frame

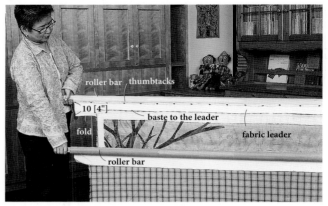

1 Use either the leaders provided by the frame company, or a 20 × 200 cm [7⅞" × 78½"] strong fabric (such as canvas). Fold it in half over the roller bars and use thumbtacks to secure it to the wood. Align and center the quilt on the fabric leader; baste, making sure it is straight. Do the same thing to the other end of the quilt.

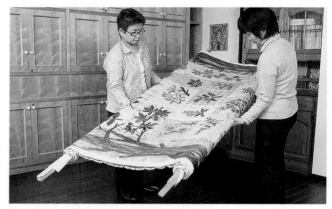

2 Having someone help you, roll the quilt over the roller bars from both sides so that the very center of the quilt (about 60 cm [23⅝"] is showing between the bars.

3 Insert the roller bars into the grooves on the quilting frame. Make 8 smaller fabric leaders, 5 × 20 cm [2" × 7⅞"] for the sides. Secure the ends to the wood of the quilt frame with thumbtacks at equal intervals (four on each side). Pin the side edges of the quilt to these side leaders so that the quilt stays taut in the frame.

6 Quilting the Quilt

1 Use a marking pencil to draw quilting lines where you want to quilt. Be careful to not use a heavy hand or very dark pencil as this might make a lighter quilting thread appear dirty. If you want to have straight lines or grids, use a ruler as you draw. If you prefer smooth, flowing lines or patterns, draw and/or quilt freehand.

2 Quilt one pattern at a time. Begin with quilting the background, followed by quilting around each appliqué and embroidery. See "Quilting Step by Step" on p. 38 and 39 for detailed directions on quilting.

3 Quilt across the entire length of the quilt in the frame, including the borders. Quilt the trunks and branches to give the appearance of bark, and freehand horizontal lines for the ground. Quilt around each of the stems, leaves, fruit and flowers in border a.

7 Binding the Quilt

Make a 3.5 cm × 760 cm [1⅜" × 8⅓ yds or 300"] of bias binding out of the homespun "Y" fabric. See p. 20 for detailed directions on making bias binding.

1 Refer to the dimensional diagram on p. 100 to draw the finished sewing line around the border.

✳ The quilting may have caused the overall project to shrink. If this is the case, it is better to adjust the width of the borders slightly than to have seam allowances less than 0.7 cm [¼"].

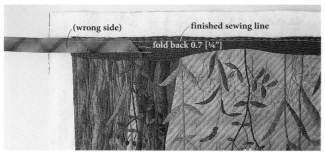

(wrong side)   finished sewing line

fold back 0.7 [¼"]

2 Start attaching the binding at the lower right of the quilt where the seams will be the least noticeable. With right sides together, place the binding on the quilt, edges together. Match the seam lines marked on the binding and the finished sewing line on the quilt and pin in place. Fold the end over 0.7 cm [¼"].

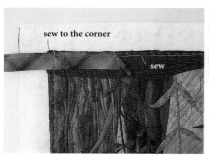

sew to the corner

sew

3 If sewing by hand, use a continuous backstitch, stitch up to the marked seam line allowance on the quilt. Then backtack with a single back-stitch to secure the stitches.

align at a 45° angle

4 Fold the binding back down and to the left, laying it along the quilt, matching edges and finished sewing lines. Using straight pins, pin the binding to the quilt, right sides together.

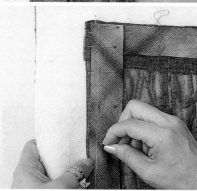

5 Insert the needle 0.7 cm [¼"] in from the edge or at the same spot where you ended in step 3, catching only the binding.

6 Using a single backstitch, backtack at the corner to secure the stitch. Turn the quilt and begin to backstitch the entire length of the side down to the next corner.

sew to the end

overlap the ends

7 Continue sewing the binding to the quilt following steps 3~6. Stitch to within a few centimeters [an inch] of where you began. Lay the binding beyond the beginning point and trim at a 45° angle, leaving 1 cm [⅜"] of overlap. Pick up the needle at the point where you stopped and continue stitching to the end of the binding.

✳ Bias binding sewn to the outside edge of the quilt before finishing.

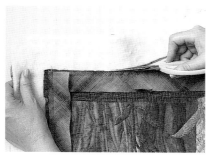

8 Laying the quilt flat, carefully trim the extra backing and batting, evening up the sides to match the edge of the sewn-on binding.

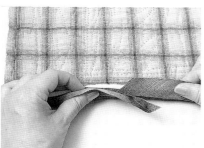

9 Turn the quilt over and finger press the binding toward the back. Overlap the beginning and ending points of the binding. Fold the binding in half to meet the edge. Then fold again over the backing so that the folded binding edge covers the stitching line. Use straight pins to pin the binding in place.

10 Using a blindstitch, stitch the binding down, being careful to cover the stitching line.

11 At each corner, fold the binding to create a perfect miter. Stitch the inner "v" area of each mitered corner to secure (don't stitch into the 45° angle). Continue stitching the binding down on each edge and mitering each corner.

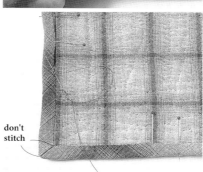

don't stitch

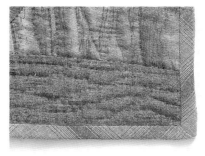

12 Finish binding the edges, ending where the binding endings overlap. This completes the quilt.

----- shown on p. 60

The Tale of Twelve Plants

✳ Finished Measurements:
174.4 × 154.4 [68¾" × 60¾"]
✳ The appliqué pattern can be found on Side A of the pattern sheet inserts.

● Materials
Cottons
  Lt print - 110 × 195 cm [43¼" × 76¾"] (center top)
  Homespun - 110 × 180 cm [43¼" × 70⅞"] (border)
  Homespun - 110 × 335 cm [43¼" × 3⅔ yds] (backing)
  Homespun - 3.5 cm × 670 cm [1⅜" × 7⅓ yds or 263¾"] (bias binding)
Batting - 110 × 335 cm [43¼" × 3⅔ yds]

In addition, 12 completed, appliquéd and embroidered main pattern blocks from the "Plants Through the Four Seasons" designs and patterns shown on p. 6~19.

Tip

The layout of the blocks on top of the center top piece is just a guide. Use the dimensional diagram as a reference, but feel free to lay out the 12 blocks you make however you like to make your own unique quilt.

● Instructions

1 Make the 12 appliquéd and embroidered blocks from the "Plants Through the Four Seasons" designs and patterns shown on p. 6~19. Be sure to make the "main pattern" designs and not the "alternate pattern" designs.

2 Referring to Fig. 1, make the patterns for borders A and B. Place the pattern on the wrong side of the border fabric, trace the outline. Reverse the pattern and trace it for the other side, so that the borders will be mirroring each other. Repeat this for the top and bottom borders. Cut them out, adding a 0.7 cm [¼"] seam allowance.

3 Cut out the center top piece. Prepare the backing fabric (Fig. 2).

4 Sew the borders together, mitering the corners. Lay the sewn borders on top of the center top piece. Pin or baste in place. Appliqué the inner edge of the border down to the center top piece using a blindstitch, turning the seam allowance under with the tip of the needle as you work (Fig. 3).

5 Turn the top over and trim away the excess fabric from the center top piece at the border seam, leaving a 1 cm [⅜"] seam allowance (Fig. 4).

6 Decide on the placement of the appliqué blocks within the center top piece. Baste in place. Turn the seam allowances under on all 4 sides of each block, blindstitch down to the center top piece using a blindstitch, turning the seam allowance under with the tip of the needle as you work. Turn the top over again and trim away the excess fabric from behind each appliquéd block, leaving a 1 cm [⅜"] seam allowance. This completes the top.

7 Layer the backing and quilt top with batting in between; baste. Quilt as desired or as shown.

8 Bind the outside edge with the bias binding and finish the quilt.

◆ Fig. 1

◆ Fig. 2

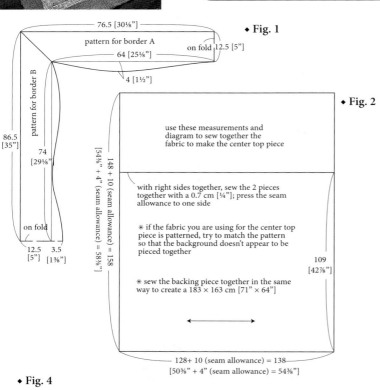

◆ Fig. 4

◆ Fig. 3

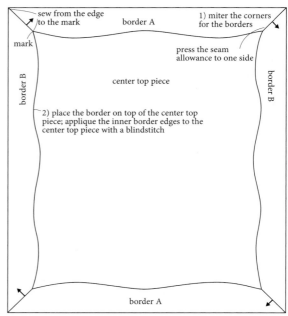

● Dimensional Diagram

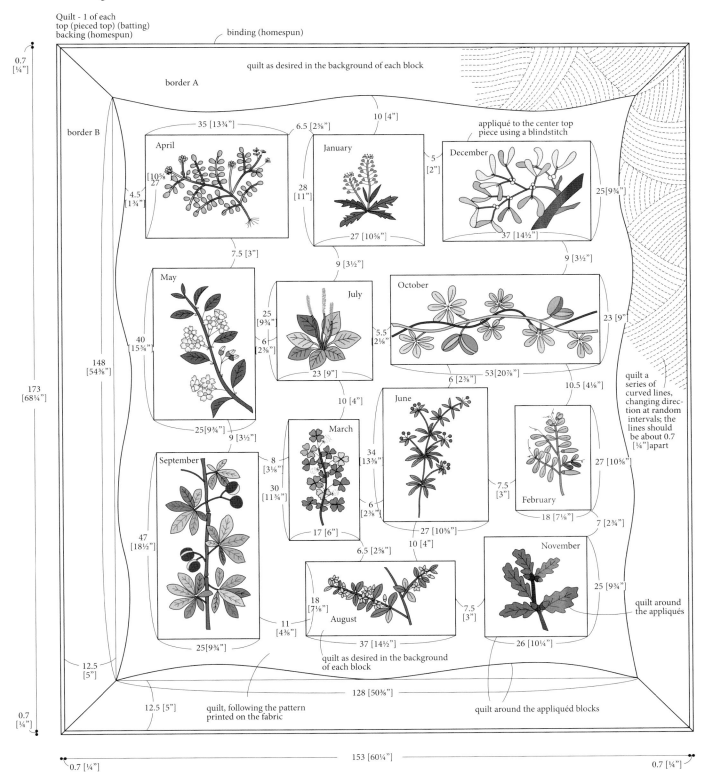

Quilt - 1 of each
top (pieced top) (batting)
backing (homespun)

binding (homespun)

0.7 [¼"]

quilt as desired in the background of each block

border A

border B

35 [13¾"]   6.5 [2⅝"]   10 [4"]

appliqué to the center top
piece using a blindstitch

April

January

5 [2"]

December

[10⅝"] 27

4.5 [1¾"]

28 [11"]

25 [9¾"]

27 [10⅝"]

37 [14½"]

7.5 [3"]

9 [3½"]

9 [3½"]

May

25 [9¾"] 6 [2⅜"]

July

October

40 [15¾"]

5.5 2⅛"

23 [9"]

148 [54⅜"]

173 [68¼"]

23 [9"]

6 [2⅜"]   53 [20⅞"]

10.5 [4⅛"]

quilt a
series of
curved lines,
changing direc-
tion at random
intervals; the
lines should
be about 0.7
[¼"] apart

25 [9¾"]   9 [3½"]

March

8 [3⅛"]

June

September

30 [11¾"]

34 13⅜"

27 [10⅝"]

February

7.5 [3"]

6 2⅜"

47 [18½"]

17 [6"]

6.5 [2⅝"]

27 [10⅝"]

10 [4"]

18 [7⅛"]

7 [2¾"]

11 [4⅜"]

August

November

25 [9¾"]

18 [7⅛"]

37 [14½"]

7.5 [3"]

25 [9¾"]

quilt around
the appliqués

12.5 [5"]

quilt as desired in the background
of each block

26 [10¼"]

0.7 [¼"]

12.5 [5"]

128 [50⅜"]

quilt, following the pattern
printed on the fabric

quilt around the appliquéd blocks

0.7 [¼"]

153 [60¼"]

0.7 [¼"]

∗ Seam allowances: add 0.7 cm [¼"] to the borders; the center top piece should be
made to 158 × 138 cm [58⅜" × 54⅜"]; the backing and batting should be made to
[71" × 64"].

111

Yoko Saito

Yoko Saito, a prominent quilt artist in Japan, is known for her exquisite designs and ingenious use of "taupe color." She teaches extensively and her work has been showcased in NHK's "Oshare Kobo" television program. Her creative works include books, block-of-the-month series in magazines and other designs sold in her shop and school, Quilt Party, which she runs.
In addition, she teaches at the NHK Culture Center, acts as the educational chief at Nihon Vogue Correspondence School and is an active member of Needlework Japan.

Quilt Party Co., Ltd.
Active Ichikawa 2-3F
1-23-2, Ichikawa, Ichikawa-shi,
Chiba-Ken, Japan 272-034

http://www.quilt.co.jp (Japanese)
http://shop.quilt.co.jp/en/index.htm (English)

Original Title	Saito Yoko no Quilt - Midori no Sampo Michi
Author	Yoko Saito
	©2009 Yoko Saito
First Edition	Originally published in Japan in 2009
Published by:	NHK Publishing, Inc.
	41-1 Udagawa-cho, Shibuya-ku,
	Tokyo, Japan 150-8081
	http://www.nhk-book.co.jp
Translation	©2013 Stitch Publications, LLC
English Translation Rights	arranged with Stitch Publications, LLC through Tuttle-Mori Agency, Inc.
Published by:	Stitch Publications, LLC
	P.O. Box 16694
	Seattle, WA 98116
	http://www.stitchpublications.com
Printed & Bound	KHL Printing, Singapore
ISBN	978-0-9859746-2-6
PCN	Library of Congress Control Number: 2012951816

Production Satomi Funamoto, Kazuko Yamada, Katsumi Mizusawa, Orie Orimi, Masue Sato, Yuko Hayashi, Keiko Nakajima, Tsuko Yamazaki, Tsuneko Shimura

Staff
Book Design	Manami Sudo
Photography	Junai Nakagawa, Yoshiharu Koizumi, Masayuki Tsutsui
Editorial Assistants	Chikami Okuda, Shikanoroom, Kumi Totsuka
Stylist	Terumi Inoue
Illustrations	Yumiko Omori
Copyeditor	Hiroko Hirochi
Editors	Jun Kobayashi (NHK Publishing)